In praise of Clare Byam-Cook and her advice

'Whenever I refer patients to Clare I am confident that, if the problem can be solved, she will solve it. Her expertise and calm, confident manner has provided help and reassurance to countless mothers over the years.'

Dr Tim Evans, Royal Physician

'Despite being a professional working with children I soon realised that, at a personal level, common sense can go out of the window. As an uncle and more recently a father I have very gratefully accepted Clare's straight-talking, no-nonsense approach. Not only do I now have a niece and son who eat and consequently sleep better, but Clare's invaluable help has resulted in four happier parents as well.'

Atul J Sabhawal, Consultant Paediatric Surgeon

'Clare really knows what she is talking about.'

Dr John Fysh, Consultant Paediatrician

'It is, for me, professionally gratifying to have a book written by someone who brings such a balanced approach to both breast- and bottle-feeding. Too often mothers are given so much differing advice as to what they should, or should not do. This book will help a new mother make her own choice and give her expert advice, which will help her with the successful feeding of her baby.'

Betty Parsons, MBE

'Thank you so much for all your advice and invaluable help in getting Charlie to take a bottle after five months of exclusive breast-feeding.'

Letter from a GP

'I'm so relieved to have Chloe on a bottle and only wish I'd been to see you months ago.'

Letter from a client

'Clare has a very balanced approach. She manages to promote breast-feeding while also taking away the guilt and feelings of inadequacy from mums who find breast-feeding not quite as "natural" as they've been led to believe.'

www.forparentsbyparents.com

Top Tips for Bottle-feeding

Clare Byam-Cook

Vermilion
LONDON

3 5 7 9 10 8 6 4

Published in 2008 by Vermilion, an imprint of Ebury Publishing

A Random House Group Company
Copyright © Clare Byam-Cook 2008

Clare Byam-Cook has asserted her right to be identified as the author of this Work in accordance with the
Copyright, Designs and Patents Act 1988

The Random House Group Limited Reg. No. 954009

Addresses for companies within the Random House Group can be found at
www.randomhouse.co.uk

A CIP catalogue record for this book is available from the British Library

The Random House Group Limited supports The Forest Stewardship Council (FSC), the leading international
forest certification organisation. All our titles that are printed on Greenpeace approved FSC certified paper carry
the FSC logo. Our paper procurement policy can be found at www.rbooks.co.uk/environment

Mixed Sources
Product group from well-managed
forests and other controlled sources
www.fsc.org   Cert no. TT-COC-2139
© 1996 Forest Stewardship Council

Printed and bound in Great Britain by
CPI Mackays, Chatham ME5 8TD

ISBN 9780091923471

Copies are available at special rates for bulk orders. Contact the sales development team
on 020 7840 8487 for more information.

To buy books by your favourite authors and register for offers, visit www.rbooks.co.uk

Contents

Acknowledgements

I would like to thank:

Christine and Peter Hill, who have advised and supported me ever since I joined Christine's practice in 1989. Both have given me the benefit of their wisdom and knowledge on all aspects of mother and baby care and they have also provided me with many of my clients! Their book *A Perfect Start* is full of sound, practical advice that will both help and reassure anxious new parents, and covers in greater detail many of the subjects that I mention in this book.

Dr John Fysh, Consultant Paediatrician at The Portland Hospital, for taking the time to discuss some of the medical aspects of this book. He also recommends me to his patients and I am grateful for his support and advice.

Author's Note

I have **not** written this book to encourage women to bottle-feed! I am very pro breast-feeding and would not want to do anything to encourage mothers to give formula rather than breast milk, but the reality is that many mothers struggle to breast-feed and end up bottle-feeding out of necessity rather than desire.

Official statistics show that 24 per cent of mothers do not even try to breast-feed (which is a great shame), and of the 76 per cent who do start breast-feeding, about 50 per cent give up within the first six weeks. Even mothers who find breast-feeding easy will usually give bottles at some point (as top-ups or when they return to work) and some mothers know in advance that they won't be able to breast-feed (because of surgery, medication etc.). I estimate that at least 98 per cent of babies are given a bottle at some point in their lives.

I think it is an absolute scandal that, despite these figures, in the drive to improve Britain's dismal breast-feeding statistics, many mothers are not given full information about bottle-feeding in their ante-natal classes. No wonder bottle-fed babies are more at risk of gastro-enteritis and obesity! Mothers need to know the correct way to sterilise bottles and make up feeds, which formula to choose and which bottle is best suited to their baby. This book will provide that information.

Because the health benefits associated with breast-feeding are so numerous (to mother as well as baby) I really do believe that every mother should give it a go. You never know, you might love it! And at least you will then be making an informed decision if you find that you can't or really don't want to breast-feed.

Having said that, I would like to point out that formula milk is not liquid poison! If you are one of the many, many mothers who find breast-feeding too difficult, you should not feel a failure or that you are harming your baby if you revert to bottle-feeding. I also firmly believe that many mothers have no choice in the matter and have to stop breast-feeding, either because they don't have enough milk or because their baby can't or won't suck efficiently.

The information in this book is for mothers whose babies are being fully formula-fed and also for mothers who are combining bottle-feeding with breast-feeding. It also covers in great detail the common problem of trying to persuade an exclusively breast-fed baby to take a bottle.

This book covers all the information you need to get started on bottle-feeding (at any age) and describes how to settle your baby and establish a good feeding pattern. I also discuss many other issues that will help you identify and resolve common medical or 'baby' problems that can affect many new babies.

Note: For simplicity and ease of writing, I refer to the baby throughout the book as 'he' and to the father of the baby as 'your husband'. This does not mean that I assume all babies are male and that everyone is married!

1 Choosing Your Bottle-feeding Equipment

There is such a bewildering choice of bottles, teats, sterilisers and other paraphernalia available in the shops that most mothers simply don't know where to begin. In addition, not all shop assistants are well informed about the merits of the different types of bottles, teats, etc., and therefore may not give you all the information you need to make an informed choice. This chapter should cover pretty much everything you could ever want or need to know about bottle-feeding equipment and will help you make decisions about what to buy. Bottle-feeding is not just a question of throwing any formula into any old bottle and then expecting your baby to feed perfectly!

Equipment
Although some equipment is absolutely essential (like bottles!), you don't have to buy everything that is on offer – for example, you don't *need* a bottle-warmer.

The main advantage in buying all the correct kit is that it will make the sterilisation and preparation of bottles easier, but the downside of buying more than you really need is that it will clutter up your kitchen and will then have to be stored until the next baby.

I suggest that you start by only getting in the essentials and then buy more things as and when you need them. Ideally you will decide which brand of products you like the best, then stick to buying within that particular range, as the products will be designed to interact with each other. For example, the Avent bottles will fit onto the Avent breast pump and will also pack perfectly into the Avent steam steriliser, but will not fit onto other pumps and vice versa.

You will need:

- six 260 ml (9 oz) bottles
- six teats
- a bottle brush
- a steam steriliser *or* sterilising solution or tablets

Note: You will not need six bottles if you are making up feeds individually and/or you begin bottle-feeding when your baby is having fewer than six feeds a day.

Bottles

There are many different types of bottle on the market and they all work. However, each manufacturer will give reasons as to why theirs is the best (e.g. by claiming to reduce the amount of air your baby will take in during feeds), so it can be quite hard to know which one to buy. Despite all the claims, I have not found that any one bottle 'works' substantially better than another but these are my tips:

- Wide-neck bottles are easier to make up feeds in than the narrow-neck bottles.
- Narrow-neck bottles will fit onto some breast pumps (e.g. Medela), so might be a better purchase if you are using these pumps.
- It might be more convenient to start off using small 150 ml (5 oz) bottles but this is unnecessary and a waste of money. The 260 ml (9 oz) bottles work just as well and you will need this size eventually anyway.
- A baby that is feeding badly or 'messily' may feed better from a different type of bottle and teat – you will need to experiment to see what suits him best.
- Some anti-colic bottles are very fiddly to clean and assemble; I would only opt for these if you establish that your baby cannot feed well from a more basic bottle.

- Disposable bottles, or bottles with disposable liners, are useful if you are travelling and can't easily sterilise. The Playtex bottle is excellent and is very economical, as you only throw away the liner rather than the whole bottle.

Note: I do not think that breast-fed babies need to be given special bottles and teats to avoid causing 'nipple/teat confusion'. But if you are breast-feeding (and giving some bottles), you should avoid using a fast-flow teat that makes it much easier for your baby to feed from the bottle than your breast. If this happens, your baby might prefer the easier option and start rejecting your breast in favour of the bottle.

Teats
Teats come in all shapes and sizes, with variable flow rates and a choice of silicone or latex. Most babies will feed well from a standard teat, but as with bottles, some teats will suit one baby better than another.

- Most wide-neck bottles can only be used with their own brand teats (e.g. you can't put a Nuk teat on an Avent bottle).
- Narrow-neck bottles are more versatile and will take any teat that is designed for narrow bottles.
- Silicone teats are more expensive than latex teats but are more durable and need replacing less often.

- Latex teats are often (but not always) softer than silicone and make feeding easier for babies with a weak suck (e.g. very premature babies).
- You can also enlarge the hole in a latex teat (using a glowing hot needle), which is useful if your baby needs a very fast flow of milk (see page 75). You can't do this with silicone teats.
- Choose a teat that is the right size for the age of your baby (this will be clearly labelled) and then experiment to see whether he likes a slow-, medium- or fast-flow teat – the medium-flow is usually a good one to start with.
- It should take your baby roughly 10–20 minutes to empty the bottle (see 'How long should each feed take?', page 27). If he takes much longer than this he needs a faster teat, and he needs a slower teat if he is feeding too fast.
- Vari-flow teats are designed to release the milk at a rate which varies according to how strongly the baby sucks. This allows the baby to feed quickly when he is very hungry and to feed more slowly at other times. This teat can also be useful when you are trying to persuade a 'lazy' baby to suck more strongly.

Sterilisers
Electric steam sterilisers will sterilise anything you put into them (breast pumps, dummies, etc.) but it's best to choose one that suits the type of bottles you are using. You will still be able to

sterilise other bottles, but they may not pack in as efficiently. Steam sterilisers are very easy to use, take between five and eight minutes to sterilise the contents, and come with clear instructions.

Microwave sterilisers work in much the same way, apart from the fact that you must own a microwave oven to operate them. They are smaller, lighter, cheaper and more portable than electric sterilisers, but will be less versatile if you regularly visit family or friends who do not have a microwave oven. They will sterilise bottles in as little as two minutes.

Sterilising fluid or tablets are useful to take away with you on holiday or when you visit friends and family to save you packing a lot of bulky sterilising equipment. You can buy a special sterilising unit or use any non-metallic container (e.g. a plastic jug, ice-cream container or Pyrex bowl), which you fill with ordinary tap water and a measure of sterilising solution or tablets. All items to be sterilised must be fully submerged in the water (you may need to use a saucer to weigh them down) and then left to soak for 15–30 minutes. The main disadvantage of this method is that the solution needs to be changed every 24 hours and the chemicals are fairly tough on your hands, which can become dry and chapped. You are also advised to rinse all items with cooled boiled water before you use them. Sterilising fluid and tablets can be bought from any chemist and come with full instructions.

Bottle-warmers

As I've already mentioned, these are not essential, as you can easily heat bottles in a jug of hot water or a microwave oven (providing you don't overheat the milk – see page 24). A bottle-warmer will often take slightly longer to heat the milk and will clutter a small kitchen – but they are useful at night if the baby's bedroom is a long way from the kitchen.

Note: A study has shown that standard feeding bottles leak a small amount of the chemical Bisphenol A (BPA) when heated. There is little evidence to show that this is harmful to babies, but it is possible for anxious parents to buy plastic bottles that are free from BPA. Glass feeding bottles are also available.

2 Which Formula Milk?

Formula milks (and breast milk) should be given to a baby for the first year as they are easier to digest and contain more suitable nutrients than cows' milk. After six months, cows' milk can be used for cooking (e.g. sauces, mashing potato etc.) but should not be given as a main drink until the baby is a year old.

There is such a wide choice of formula milks on offer that it can be hard to know which to choose. In addition to the normal milks, there are specialist formula milks for babies who have milk allergies or intolerance, reflux, as well as for pre-term babies and hungrier babies etc.

But first things first:

- Paediatricians tell me that they do not recommend any particular brand. They all contain similar ingredients and it is only good marketing that persuades a mother she is giving her baby 'the best' formula milk. Nor do they recommend organic over non-organic.

- It is, however, best to choose a brand that contains added prebiotics (which are a natural component of breast milk), as these will increase the friendly bacteria in the baby's gut and help develop his immune system.
- If the formula you choose doesn't appear to agree with your baby (i.e. he brings quite a lot of it up, becomes 'mucusy' or just won't drink much), it's worth swapping to another brand to see whether it suits him better.
- If this doesn't help, don't continue to try other brands as there might be another cause (such as reflux or milk allergy) for his symptoms. See your doctor and take his advice.
- If there is a strong family history of allergies, it might be best to use a hypo-allergenic formula right from the outset, but you should also discuss this with your doctor first. It's not a good idea to label your baby as 'allergic' without first getting a medical opinion.
- Consult your GP or paediatrician before using *any* specialist milk – this is because many doctors think that some milks (e.g. soya) can cause worse problems than the standard cows' milk formulas.
- Ready-made milks (in cartons and small bottles) are nutritionally the same as making up your own with powder, but are a lot more expensive!

Regardless of which brand of formula you choose, make sure that it is suitable for the age of your baby, and only graduate to milk for the older or 'hungrier' baby once it becomes appropriate.

Each tin of formula milk will have full instructions on making up the feeds and storage, and will also include feeding guidelines as to roughly how much milk your baby will need according to his age and weight. Do be aware that this is only an approximate guide. As long as his weight gain is good, it doesn't matter if he is drinking more or less than the chart recommends.

First infant milk
This should be your first choice of milk for a normal healthy baby and is suitable from birth. It will be whey dominant, meaning it is easy to digest and as close to breast milk as possible.

Milk for the 'hungrier' baby
This can also be used from birth, but is casein (rather than whey) dominant. Casein is harder to digest than whey, which means the milk stays in a baby's stomach for longer and leaves him feeling more satisfied and better able to feed slightly less frequently. It is *not* more fattening than other milks and is ideal to use for a hungry baby who is feeding frequently and gaining too much weight. You should only switch to this milk if your baby clearly needs it, because a very young baby might find it too hard to digest, and this will make him uncomfortable and unsettled.

Follow-on milk
You should switch to this milk at six months. In addition to all the previous ingredients, follow-on milks contain extra iron, calcium and Vitamin D, all of which are beneficial for older babies. In addition to solid food, this will meet all his nutritional needs until he can start drinking ordinary cows' milk at the age of one year.

Specialist formula milks
These are designed for babies with special dietary needs (e.g. pre-term or low-birth-weight babies, and babies with milk allergies etc.), or those with feeding problems (such as reflux) who need to use a specialist rather an ordinary formula milk. Many of these are available on prescription only, but others can be bought over the counter. None the less, I really do recommend that you consult a doctor before using any of these milks (including soya and goats' milk) to be sure that:

- your baby is genuinely unable to drink cows' milk formula
- a proper diagnosis is made (e.g. of milk allergy) so the right milk is prescribed and follow-up appointments are made to review your baby's progress

3 Sterilising Bottles and Making Up Feeds

Most mothers are aware of the importance of sterilising feeding equipment, though few fully appreciate why it needs to be done. Once it is all explained, a mother will become much more confident about her own ability to decide what needs sterilising, how often, and when she can stop sterilising altogether.

You need to sterilise because:

- young babies are very susceptible to germs
- milk is a perfect medium in which germs can multiply
- sterilising is the best way to ensure that germs are destroyed

Although mothers are told that they must sterilise all feeding equipment for a minimum of six months, it is in fact safe to use something that has not been sterilised **providing you have washed it properly** (see page 16). After all, a mother does not pop her breast into a steriliser before it goes into her baby's mouth!

These are the basic principles of hygiene and sterilising:

- You should wash your hands before allowing your baby to suck on your finger but, having washed your hands once, you do not need to wash them again unless you do something that might contaminate them, such as a nappy change.
- You do not need to be fanatical about washing every time you touch something, but you should wash your hands very carefully after handling raw meat, going to the loo etc.
- A dummy that falls out of your baby's mouth into his cot can be put straight back into his mouth, but if it falls onto a dirty street it should not be used again until it has been sterilised (or washed very thoroughly if you don't have a spare one to hand). Putting the dummy in your own mouth and sucking on it does not make it germ-free and safe to go back in the baby's mouth.
- If a bottle is not *completely* clean when you fill it with milk, any bacteria it contains will start multiplying at such a rate that by the time you give the feed there may be enough present to give your baby a tummy upset. A minor tummy upset is unlikely to do much harm, but if there's a particularly nasty bug in the bottle, your baby could suffer severe gastro-enteritis and might need to be admitted to hospital.

- If you need a bottle in a hurry (and don't have time to sterilise), it should be safe to wash the bottle thoroughly, fill it with milk and use it immediately. Any bacteria that might be left inside would not have a chance to multiply to a dangerous level in such a short time.

Washing before sterilising

Sterilising is not a substitute for washing, so everything must be washed thoroughly before you sterilise it. Bottles, teats, etc., should be rinsed in cold water immediately after use and then left soaking until you are ready to wash them all in one go – this makes washing quicker and easier.

- Fill a sink with hot soapy water and use a bottle-brush to wash each bottle really thoroughly, inside and out, making sure that you brush around the ridges of the bottle and its screw-top.
- Teats can be washed by squirting a bit of neat washing-up liquid into them and then giving them a good squidge around (both inside and out) using your fingers. You can also use a small brush especially designed for washing teats.
- Rinse with clean water and put all items straight into the steriliser – you do not need to dry them first.
- The bottle brush does not need to be sterilised, but should be kept in a clean place, e.g. in a jam jar (which you should also wash regularly).

Everything you wash (but are not planning to sterilise) should be left to drip-dry on a clean rack or paper towel – or you can shake the water off and use it immediately. If you use a grubby drying-up cloth or put items to drain on a dirty work surface, you will immediately contaminate them and make them unsafe to use.

Note: In the USA, many mothers put all their baby-feeding equipment in the dishwasher and do not sterilise any of it. This is less safe to do here, because dishwashers in the UK wash at a lower temperature than they do in the USA.

Sterilising methods

You can use an electric or microwave steam steriliser, or sterilise in cold water using liquid or tablets (see page 6) following the manufacturer's instructions.

You can also sterilise items by boiling them in a saucepan. The bottles should be immersed in cold water (making sure there are no air bubbles left inside the bottles) and then boiled for at least 10 minutes. The teats can be added for the last three minutes but be aware that they will perish quickly if you boil them too often.

Note: Pouring boiling water over a teat, dummy, etc., does *not* sterilise it.

How long will equipment remain sterile?

Most manufacturers say that the contents need re-sterilising every time you open the steriliser to get something out. This is being overly cautious! If you wash your hands carefully before removing items from the steriliser, everything left will remain safe to use for about 24 hours. But if your hands are dirty and/or you sneeze into the steriliser before replacing the lid, you will need to wash and sterilise again! Bottles that are removed from the steriliser and kept fully assembled with their lids on will remain sterile for about 24 hours, even when left at room temperature in the kitchen or out and about with you and the baby. These bottles can be left empty or filled with cooled boiled water – but if you put milk into them, they should be kept cool in the fridge.

Making up feeds

Current advice is that bottles should be made up immediately before a feed, rather than being prepared in advance and kept stored in the fridge. This is another example of manufacturers being overly cautious! Mothers are advised to make up one feed at a time simply to make allowances for those who fail to sterilise and/or store the feeds correctly – the milk does not start deteriorating once the powder is added.

You can therefore decide which suits you the best; preparing 24 hours' worth of feeds in advance or waiting until your baby is hungry before mixing the milk.

These are the pros and cons:

Method one: preparing in advance

- I think it is quicker and more efficient to get into the habit of making up all the feeds at the same time each day rather than doing each individual bottle as and when you need it.
- Your crying, hungry baby doesn't have to wait while you prepare his bottle.
- Bottles of milk must be kept cool, which means taking a cool bag when you are out for the day, travelling etc.
- The milk has to be warmed before you give it – easy and quick if you microwave it, but slower if you don't.

Method two: making individual bottles

- Can be stressful if your baby is screaming for his feed. Anyone can get a bottle out of the fridge for you, but not everyone (e.g. a visiting friend) will know how to find and add the powder in a hurry.
- When out and about, you have to take bottles and powder with you in separate containers.
- You can keep the bottle filled with water at room temperature – no need for cool bags and possibly no need to heat the bottle either. (See page 24, 'Warming the milk'.)
- Safer if you are not meticulous with hygiene and sterilising.

- No chance of your baby being given old milk that has been left at the back of the fridge for a week (or longer).

When making up the feeds you should:

- Rinse out the kettle, fill it with water (taken from the cold water tap) and bring it to the boil.
- Allow the water to cool for about 10 minutes (so that the water is still hot, but not boiling).
- Wash your hands, take the bottles out of the steriliser and stand them on a clean work surface.
- Fill the bottles with the correct amount of water – i.e. 180 ml (6 oz) of water if you want to make up 180 ml (6 oz) of milk.
- Add the milk powder to the water, first checking the tin for instructions as to how much powder to add. It is usually one level scoop of powder per 30 ml (1 oz) of water.
- Dissolve the powder by putting the tops back on the bottles and giving them a really good shake.
- Put bottles straight into the fridge, even though they will be quite hot. (The sooner you cool the milk down, the sooner you will stop germs multiplying if you have failed to sterilise the bottles correctly.)
- You can leave the bottles out of the fridge if you are not adding powder to the water.

Do not:

- Use mineral water, as this is designed for adults, not babies (unless the label specifically states that it is suitable for babies).
- Use water that has been softened (i.e. if you have a water softener in your house).
- Boil the water more than once as this concentrates the chemicals in the water.
- Add more than the recommended amount of powder.
- Use milk that is more than 24 hours old – all old milk must be thrown away.
- Put a half-finished bottle of milk in the fridge to be used again later in the day. (This is unhygienic and can allow harmful bacteria to multiply.)

Note: It is only necessary to use bottled (rather than tap) water in countries where the water is not considered to be safe to drink, and you should always boil the water, regardless of whether you are using tap or bottled water.

How much milk to offer
It's impossible to be precise about exactly how much milk should be given as all babies' needs differ. However, as a rough guide, most babies under the age of four months will need approximately 150 ml

(5o z) of milk per kg of body weight (or 2½–3 oz per lb) during each 24-hour period. To work out how much your baby will need at each feed, you divide the total amount of milk he needs by the number of feeds he is having.

Metric
For a 3 kg baby on six feeds a day, you would multiply 3 kg by 150 ml = 450 ml. Divided by six feeds = 75 ml per feed.

Imperial
For a 7 lb baby on seven feeds a day, you should multiply 7 lb by 3 oz = 21 oz. Divided by seven feeds = 3 oz per feed.

As this is only a rough guide (because I have multiplied by 3 oz, rather than by 2½ oz) you should not worry if your baby takes slightly more or less than this.

- Always make up a bit more than you think your baby needs so that if he is particularly hungry at one feed he can have more.
- There should always be a small amount of milk left in the bottle at the end of each feed, so you can be fairly sure that he has stopped feeding because he has had enough milk, rather than because there was no more milk available to him.

● A bottle-fed baby tends to take pretty much the same amount of milk at each feed, but his appetite will vary a little. Don't force him to drink more when he has clearly had enough, as this is likely to make him gain too much weight.

4 Feeding Your Baby

When your baby wakes for his feed, you should change his nappy, warm his milk (see overleaf) and then settle down to give him the bottle. If you are using the correct teat, your baby should feed calmly and steadily, and take roughly 10–20 minutes to finish his bottle. He then needs winding, swaddling and settling down to sleep.

Changing nappies

This needs to be done at every feed time and whenever he has a dirty nappy. This will keep your baby comfortable and prevent nappy rash. Ideally you would change the nappy before a feed (so that you can settle your baby after the feed without disturbing him), but it may be better to change his nappy in the middle or end of a feed if:

- He is screaming with hunger and wants to be fed immediately.
- He regularly opens his bowels during feeds – it is a waste of time and money to change his nappy twice.
- He often falls asleep before he has had enough milk – changing his nappy is an effective way of waking him enough to finish his feed.

Warming the milk
Although some babies are perfectly happy to drink cold milk taken straight from the fridge, most babies feed better if you warm the milk. You can do this by:

- Standing the bottle in a jug of recently boiled water – this will heat the bottle more quickly than using hot water from a tap.
- Using a thermostatically controlled bottle-warmer available from most baby shops.
- Using a microwave. This is perfectly safe providing you do not overheat the milk (which may destroy some of the nutrients) or give it too hot (which may burn your baby). When using a microwave, you will need to experiment to see how many seconds it takes to warm the milk to the correct temperature – this will depend on the amount of milk that you are heating as well as the power of your microwave oven. It's best to heat the bottle with the lid off and you should shake it well to disperse any hot spots.

All the above methods are fine, but you *must* check the temperature of the milk before giving it to your baby. You can do this by shaking a few drops onto the back of your hand – the milk should feel warm but not hot. A baby's mouth is very sensitive and easily burnt so, if in doubt, give the milk slightly too cold rather than slightly too hot.

It's also well worth varying the temperature of the milk you give your baby as some babies can become very fussy and start refusing the milk if it is not always at exactly the temperature they are used to.

Note: If your baby's bedroom is a long way from the kitchen, and you don't have a bottle-warmer, you can save time at night by taking a vacuum flask of hot water (to heat the bottle) upstairs with you when you go to bed. The milk can also be taken upstairs and kept cool in a cool bag.

Giving the feed

Choose a chair (or bed) that allows you to sit comfortably, so that both you and your baby can relax and enjoy the feed.

- Hold your baby with his head tilted slightly back over your arm – if he is too scrunched up you will find it harder to put the teat in his mouth and he will find it harder to swallow.
- You should hold your baby in a slightly more upright position than you would if you were breast-feeding – this ensures that he won't choke on the milk (if it flows too fast) and also helps the wind to come up as he feeds.
- The teat should go straight into his mouth (i.e. not at an angle) – if it goes in crookedly, it will be harder for his mouth to form a seal around the teat and he may swallow more air as he feeds.

- Hold the bottle so that the teat is always completely filled with milk – you will need to tilt your baby slightly further back as the bottle empties so he doesn't swallow air instead of milk.
- When the baby stops sucking, you should wind him (see page 28) and then offer him more milk.
- When he rejects the bottle he is probably full.

Bottle-feeding is easy when a baby feeds well and only stops sucking when he has had enough milk. Unfortunately this doesn't always happen! It may take several feeds or even several days to discover whether your baby is giving you the right signals, but it is fairly simple: if he settles well and gains weight he is getting it right. If he is slow to settle and/or is not gaining enough weight, he probably needs more milk. It may help to know that:

- A small baby with a weak suck can get tired and fall asleep before he has drunk all the milk he needs.
- Although most babies who are still hungry open their mouths every time the bottle touches their lips, some don't.
- Babies don't always need exactly the same amount of milk at every feed, so it can be hard to judge when your baby has had enough.
- If you are using too slow a teat (so the feed takes too long), your baby may lose his appetite before he has had enough milk. Or the reverse can happen – if he feeds too quickly he may take in so

much air that he is difficult to wind and too uncomfortable to finish the feed.

- You may need to experiment to find out which teat and which milk flow works best for your baby.
- If your baby doesn't last as long between feeds whenever he has taken significantly less milk than usual, you could try to get him to take a little bit more milk.
- The best way to judge whether your baby is getting the right amount of milk is to weigh him regularly – if he is putting on too much or too little weight you should adjust the amount of milk that you offer him.

Note: If you have a very hungry baby who is not satisfied for long between feeds, you could offer him formula milk designed for the hungrier baby to see whether this helps.

How long should each feed take?
It should take your baby about 10–20 minutes to drink his bottle, regardless of how old he is and how much milk is in the bottle. This is because the strength of a baby's suck is normally in proportion to his size – a big baby will finish a large feed in roughly the same time that a small baby will finish a small feed.

However, two babies of a similar age and weight may vary hugely in how efficiently they feed; one may suck strongly and continuously until he has finished the bottle, while the other may have a much weaker suck and keep falling asleep throughout the feed. It doesn't matter if your baby feeds very quickly (less than 10 minutes) or very slowly (more than 20 minutes) providing he enjoys the feed (i.e. he is not choking and taking in too much air) and is getting enough milk.

Note: If you are struggling to find a teat that enables him to feed at a reasonable rate, see 'Can't or won't suck efficiently', page 65.

How many feeds a day?

A healthy normal baby needs to feed roughly three- to four-hourly for the first six weeks or so – this means he will have between six and nine feeds every 24 hours. As he gets older and starts sleeping longer at night (hopefully at around six weeks), he will gradually reduce this to between five and six feeds a day. Once he is sleeping right through the night he may only need four or five feeds a day. You may need to feed your baby more frequently than this (i.e. at least three-hourly) if he is premature, very small, jaundiced or suffering from a problem such as reflux.

Winding

When a baby feeds, he will usually swallow some air, which then starts accumulating in his tummy as wind. The more air he takes in, the more uncomfortable he will feel and the more frequently he will need winding. A very small proportion of babies do not suffer from wind at all, but the vast majority do need winding once or twice both during and after a feed. Your baby will normally let you know when he needs to be winded (by stopping feeding and/or crying), so you can generally allow him to carry on sucking for as long as he wants and only wind him when he stops feeding or seems to be uncomfortable.

You should always wind a baby at the end of a feed and also at any point during a feed when he seems uncomfortable. You need to do this for the following reasons:

- A baby with too much wind in his tummy can become too uncomfortable to carry on feeding.
- Air in his tummy can sometimes make him feel full and stop him feeding before he has had enough milk.
- Winding a baby firmly will usually wake him up if he has fallen asleep before he has had enough milk – a baby will often doze off when his tummy is only half-full.
- If your baby does wake up when you wind him, you should offer him the bottle again to see whether he wants more milk.
- Winding a baby at the end of each feed is essential because a baby will rarely settle for long if he still has wind in his tummy. Even a baby who appears to be sound asleep will tend to wake and start crying within minutes if you lie him down without first winding him.

Note: If your baby brings up a lot of milk when you only wind him at the end of the feed, try winding him earlier to see whether you can avoid this happening. It doesn't matter if he brings up a lot of milk but if he brings up too much you may then need to replace some of it by feeding him a bit more, and this can become rather time-consuming.

How to wind your baby
The air bubbles trapped in a baby's tummy will only be able to come up easily if his back is straight. The three main ways to wind a baby are:

1. Hold his body firmly against your chest with one hand and use the other hand to push gently into the small of his back to make sure it is completely straight. His back will normally feel stiff when he does have wind and relaxed and flexible when he doesn't. This is my favourite method.

Winding: holding baby against chest

2. Sit your baby on your lap, leaning him slightly forward, supporting his head with your hand while you pat his back. This works perfectly well, but you must make sure that he doesn't sit in a crumpled heap with his back bent – it will take much longer to wind him if his back isn't straight.

3. Lay him over your shoulder while you pat or rub his back. This works well (as it does ensure that his back is straight) but it can be a bit messy if your baby sicks up a lot of milk onto your clothes! Although it is very common and normal for a baby to bring up a small amount of milk when he burps (this is called 'possetting'), he is more likely to bring up milk when there is pressure on his tummy.

Winding in the middle of a feed is not essential, so don't insist on doing this if your baby gets agitated and clearly wants to get on with feeding. Once the feed is over, you should spend a maximum of ten (but normally only two to three) minutes winding your baby – if he hasn't brought up wind within this time it's probably not worth carrying on.

How will I know whether I have got all the wind up?
The short answer is – you won't! It is really a question of trial and error at first because you cannot assume that once a baby has done one burp there are no more to come. However, as you get to know your baby, you will discover for yourself whether he never needs winding, whether he is fully winded after only one burp or whether it

takes several burps before all his wind is up. Remember: if his back is floppy and relaxed he is unlikely to have wind.

Hiccups

It is very common for a baby to have hiccups. Most babies are completely untroubled by them and will happily carry on with whatever they are doing – feeding, sleeping etc. But if your baby *is* unsettled with hiccups, you could try offering him some cool boiled water (either from a bottle or from a spoon) to see if this helps.

Settling your baby after a feed

Some babies are very easy to settle; others are not. However, a baby will normally sleep longer and better when swaddled, so ask a midwife, relative or friend to show you how to do this. Most babies feel secure with their whole body firmly swaddled, but if your baby clearly hates having his arms confined and/or he wants to suck his thumb, you can wrap him up leaving his arms free.

Don't risk overheating your baby (use a cotton sheet and fewer clothes and blankets in hot weather) and always put him down to sleep on his back or his side but *not* on his tummy (because of the risk of cot death, see page 43).

- Your baby may fall asleep immediately or he may gaze around for a bit before dozing off. Either is fine!

- If he starts grizzling or crying gently, leave him for a while to see whether he settles – it's not unkind to do this as many babies will only fall asleep if they are left to cry. If you keep picking up a crying baby you may end up making him thoroughly overtired and even more incapable of going to sleep.

- If he is still awake after about 10 minutes but his crying is at the same level or diminishing, you can leave him for a little bit longer. You could also offer him a dummy (see overleaf), rock his crib and/or gently pat his back.

- If his crying escalates and he is clearly becoming more unsettled, you should pick him up to wind him again and calm him down.

- If absolutely nothing (i.e. winding, rocking or dummy) settles him, you need to go back to square one and offer him more milk.

Once all his needs have been met, a baby will normally fall asleep quite quickly and stay asleep until the next feed is due. But if your baby is always really hard to settle see 'The unsettled baby', page 86.

Note: For the first few weeks most babies fall sound asleep after a feed and then demand to be fed as soon as they wake up. After about four to six weeks, babies start becoming more alert, need less sleep and spend more time awake and playing. At this point, they will either still go straight to sleep after a feed but not need to be fed when they first wake up; or remain happily awake after a feed for quite some time before going to sleep, but then want to be fed the instant they wake up.

Dummies

Opinion is divided on the use of dummies. In general they are frowned upon as prolonged and excessive use is thought to have an adverse effect on a child's speech and intelligence, but conversely, more recent research suggests that using a dummy reduces cot deaths.

Personally, I loathe them, but none the less I do think that a dummy can be an invaluable aid when it comes to settling some babies and I will happily suggest using one when necessary.

I recommend that you:

- Do not use a dummy on a baby who can't go to sleep because he is still hungry.
- Only use a dummy if you cannot settle your baby without one. Don't automatically put it in his mouth every time you put him down to sleep – wait and see if he can settle without it.
- Don't use it just to stop your baby crying (e.g. when you are changing his nappy).
- Don't use a dummy when you are walking your baby in a pram or buggy, as the movement should be enough to rock him to sleep.

If you follow these guidelines, your baby is unlikely to become addicted to the dummy and will usually stop using it of his own accord once he no longer needs it. This normally happens at about three months when a baby either stops needing something to suck on before going to sleep, or he discovers his thumb and uses that instead.

Note: Dummies need to be washed and sterilised frequently. Putting the dummy in your own mouth and sucking on it does not make it germ-free and safe to go back in your baby's mouth – this particularly applies if you have a cold or any other infection, which may then be transmitted to your baby.

Feeding twins

Bottle-feeding twins is potentially harder than breast-feeding twins because it is more difficult to feed them simultaneously when using bottles rather than breasts. On the other hand, bottle-feeding has the advantage of a limitless supply of milk, and others can help you with the feeds. If possible, arrange to have someone to help you in the early weeks as it can be very tiring and stressful trying to feed, wind and settle two babies on your own. Although some mothers manage amazingly well right from the word go, they are the exception, so don't feel demoralised if you can't cope on your own.

What to expect:

- Most twins are delivered earlier than their due date and are likely to be smaller (and possibly slightly weaker) than a full-term single baby. Very small twins may need to be admitted to the neonatal intensive care unit initially – your midwives will explain everything to you if this happens.

- Don't worry if your babies need to stay a few extra days in hospital in order to get feeding established, check for jaundice etc. It is better to know that the babies are feeding well and taking enough milk before you leave hospital than to start worrying about it at home.

- You may initially be given strict guidelines as to how much and how frequently the babies need to be fed. These guidelines will become more relaxed once everyone is sure that the babies are gaining the right amount of weight.

Once you are home, it is best to try to synchronise feeds so that the twins feed and sleep at the same time. This way you will have time in between feeds to look after yourself – sleeping, eating and resting are very important for your health and well-being. This is obviously much easier to achieve if you have help (husband, mother or maternity nurse). If you are on your own, I think you should plan to feed the babies one after the other so that each baby has your full attention and is cuddled as he feeds. Your babies will enjoy this far more than being bottle-fed propped up by cushions.

The aim is to give each baby enough milk to last until the next feed, which ideally would be three to four hours later. The timing of the next feed is then dictated by the baby who wakes the first; if he needs to feed after three hours, it would be wrong to make him wait for his brother to be hungry. Instead, you should wake the sleeping twin and try to feed them both together – most babies are happy to be fed earlier rather than later, so this normally works very well. But if this always upsets the sleeping twin, who then feeds badly and is slow to settle again, you may need to allow them to feed at separate times. It is usually possible to get the babies synchronised at some stage, so don't worry if you can't manage it in the early weeks.

Hygiene

It is important to be meticulous about hygiene as it is easy to spread germs between two babies. You don't need to wash your hands in between handling one baby and the other during feed times, but you should wash your hands after nappy changes, before preparing bottles etc., just as you would if you only had one baby.

- The babies should not suck from the same bottle or share a dummy. Using different-coloured rings on the bottles will help avoid confusion.
- If one baby has an infection (e.g. thrush in his mouth) you must wash and sterilise everything very thoroughly and you should also wash your hands carefully after you handle that baby.
- If either baby develops an infection or a minor illness such as a cold, you should keep them apart until the ill one is better.

Most twins like to be physically close to each other and will usually settle better if they are put to sleep in the same cot. But if one twin keeps being disturbed and woken by the other, it is better to separate them than to have two wakeful babies!

5 The First Few Days

Life with a new baby can be daunting as well as exciting. Ideally you would have someone (e.g. your husband or mother) to stay with you for the first two weeks or so, until you have got used to the responsibility of caring for your baby on your own. During this time you should:

- rest as much as possible
- keep visitors to a minimum
- share the care of your baby – you don't have to do everything to be a good mother!

Plan ahead
Well before your baby is due, you should unpack all your feeding equipment, read the relevant instructions and make sure that both you and your husband know how it all works. Your baby may want to feed as soon as you get home from the hospital and you will quickly get stressed if he is crying for food and you don't know how to prepare his bottle. Ideally your husband will get everything set up

before he collects you from hospital so that at least one bottle is available for immediate use. You may want to use cartons of ready-made formula for the first few feeds until you get fully organised.

When your baby is born
Most babies want to feed very shortly after the birth and your midwife will advise you when he is ready. She will give you a bottle of ready-made formula (which does not need warming) and your baby will almost certainly know how to suck and take as much milk as he wants. He should then settle quickly to sleep. This is what to expect:

- He will only drink small amounts at first – about 10–30 ml (less than 1 oz) – and will gradually increase his intake as he starts needing more. Let him decide how much he wants.
- If he swallowed a lot of amniotic fluid during the birth he may be a bit 'mucusy' and vomit back some of the milk. This is normal and he will stop doing this once he has cleared his stomach – usually within 24 hours.
- He may not want to feed much within the first 24 hours but after this he should feed roughly every three to four hours.
- You should offer him a new bottle at each feed – do not keep using the same bottle until he has finished it. This is unhygienic and potentially harmful as it allows bacteria to multiply.

- If he is getting enough milk he should settle well after feeds and have at least six wet nappies a day.

Note: If you give birth at home all of the above still applies, apart from the fact that you will have to provide your own bottles of formula.

Rest

Giving birth is tiring and you need time to recover. Try to relax when you first get home rather than rushing around catching up on housework, cooking etc. Allow others to help, and try to fit in a daytime nap.

Visitors

It's very exciting having a new baby to show off, but don't overdo it! Having lots of visitors will not only make you very tired, but might also unsettle your baby if he is forever being cuddled (or photographed) when he should be feeding or sleeping. A baby that is overtired or made to wait too long for feeds will soon become unsettled and you may set the trend for disruptive days and nights.

Of course you will want family and close friends to come and see your baby, but it is a good idea to agree with your husband in advance how long you want them to stay. He can then be the one to ask them to leave if they are staying too long. Many visitors think that they should stay a long time in order to show sufficient interest in the new baby, so it is helpful for them (as well as you), to know how long the visit should last.

Midwives and health visitors

All mothers and babies must be seen regularly by a community midwife for the first 10 days after the birth, after which time she hands over to a health visitor. The midwife should visit you within 24 hours of you coming home, agree when she will next come to see you, and give you her contact details if you need to see or speak to her earlier than that. Her role is to check your health and make sure that your uterus is contracting back down after the birth. She will also carry out routine tests on your baby, weigh him, and advise you if you are having feeding or any other problems. If she thinks it necessary, she may carry on visiting you beyond day 10.

Your health visitor will usually call on or around day 10. She will give you a booklet in which to keep records of your baby's development, weight etc., and tell you where your nearest baby clinic is and how to get hold of her should you need to. She is the one who will give you more general advice on babycare, check that your baby is reaching his milestones, and tell you when he needs his injections, hearing tests etc.

6 Caring For Your New Baby

This chapter covers all the basic questions I am asked by new parents, who worry about all sorts of things when they come home from the hospital: where the baby should sleep; how warm their house needs to be; how much help is needed and/or advisable.

Cot death
This is a major source of concern for new parents. Cot deaths have dropped dramatically with the 'back to sleep' campaign and research continues to throw more light on the subject, with advice often changing as a result. For example, several childcare specialists have made a great point of recommending co-sleeping, but recent research has now shown that it is not advisable to have your baby sleeping in bed with you.

It is currently recommended that:

- The safest place for a baby to sleep is in a cot in the parents' bedroom for the first six months.

- A baby is laid on his back to sleep, not on his tummy.
- Your baby's head is left uncovered in his cot. You should lie him down with his feet touching the end of the cot – to prevent him slipping under the blankets.
- Do not let anyone smoke near your baby. Parents who smoke anywhere in the house put their baby at a greater risk than non-smokers.
- You should not let your baby get too hot.
- You do not let your baby sleep in bed with you, especially if you smoke, have been drinking alcohol or are taking medication that makes you sleepy.
- You should not feed your baby in bed if you are so tired that you might fall asleep.
- You should not sleep with your baby on a sofa or armchair.

If you can follow all the above suggestions, your baby will be receiving the best possible care and you should try not to become too anxious about anything untoward happening to him.

Where your baby should sleep
Although research has shown that it is best to put a baby to sleep in a separate cot, some childcare experts continue to disagree with this and think that co-sleeping with your baby is both safe and an important part of mother–baby bonding. They believe that a baby

needs to remain close to his mother in order to feel secure and loved, and that it is wrong to deprive him of this comfort.

I completely disagree! I think that **a normal, healthy baby, who has had all his needs met, will sleep soundly and happily wherever you put him**. But if he does *not* sleep happily in his cot, you may not have met all his needs, in which case you need to find out what the problem is and sort it. If you take him into bed with you without addressing the problem (e.g. hunger, wind) you will probably succeed in stopping him crying, but this is not the best way to resolve the issue – *and* it goes against current safety guidelines.

I say this because:

- If a baby is still hungry or needs winding, all you have to do is meet these needs and he will happily go to sleep.
- If you can never find a way to stop him crying other than to cuddle him, you should consult a health professional to see whether he has a medical problem (e.g. reflux) that needs treating.
- There is strong evidence to suggest that it *is* risky to sleep with your baby.
- If your baby becomes accustomed to sleeping with you, this will almost certainly prove to be a hard habit to break when you eventually decide that you want him to sleep in his own bed.

The next issue is whether your baby should sleep in the same room as you or separately in his own room. From a safety point of view, it is ideal to keep him in your bedroom, but this may not suit all parents for a number of reasons:

- A small bedroom may not have enough space for a cot.
- If you are a light sleeper, you will wake with all his little baby noises rather than only being woken when he actually needs attention.
- If you are a noisy sleeper, you might find that you are waking your baby, rather than him waking you!
- Both you *and* your husband will be woken at feed times. This is fine if your husband wants to be fully involved, but not if he has to go to work in the morning. It's not very practical to have both of you suffering from a lack of sleep. You at least should be able to catch up on lost sleep with a daytime nap.

Other useful tips

- If your baby sleeps in a separate room, you should use a baby monitor if he is out of earshot.
- During the day, your baby can sleep anywhere that suits you, so long as you can see or hear him.
- During the first few weeks a baby does not need quiet or darkness to keep him asleep, and he will not normally be

disturbed by all that is going on around him. But if you always tuck him away in an upstairs bedroom and creep around whenever he is sleeping, he will become used to total silence and is then more likely to wake every time the phone rings, a doorbell goes or any other unexpected noise happens.

- It may also help your baby to distinguish between night and day if, right from the start, you only put him to sleep in his bedroom at night. However, once you notice that he *is* beginning to become a bit more sensitive to noise, he may sleep longer and better during his naps if you put him to sleep in his bedroom with the curtains drawn. This usually happens after about three months.
- Fresh air is good for babies and encourages sleep. Whenever possible it's good to put your baby to sleep outside in a pram – he should be within sight or earshot, appropriately dressed and using a cat net when necessary. You can also open the windows in his bedroom when he is having his daytime naps.

Babies tend to sleep longer and more soundly when lying flat than they do when sitting up in a baby seat. Leaving a baby to cat nap in his bouncing chair or keeping him in the car seat when you arrive at your destination will usually cause him to wake sooner than he would if you settle him in his Moses basket.

Room temperature

When you first take your baby home your house will need to be warmer than usual but not as hot as it was in hospital – a house temperature of about 18–20°C is ideal. It will not harm your baby if you keep your house cooler than this, but it might seem a bit chilly when you are changing his nappy, bathing him etc.

Many mothers are so obsessive about room temperature that they keep a thermometer near their baby's cot and then panic if the temperature varies by a degree or two. You do not need to do this! There is no point in being this precise unless you also know exactly how many clothes your baby should be wearing at each degree of the temperature gauge. Instead, be guided by common sense and adjust his clothing according to his surroundings – your baby is not as fragile as you might think and will only be at risk if you get it so completely wrong that he is far too hot or freezing cold. His body should always feel nice and warm, and you can use mittens and bootees if his hands and feet get a bit chilly.

During the winter months you should ensure that his room does not get too cold at night when the central heating goes off – cold is a common cause of a baby waking at night, especially as he gets older and starts wriggling out from under his blankets. The most economical way to keep your baby's room warm is to use a convector heater or an electric radiator with thermostatic controls. Remember, your baby will get cold more quickly than you will, partly because he is so small and partly because he is not generating heat by moving around as an adult does.

Note: Whenever I come across a mother who is still overly anxious about whether her house is too warm or too cold, I ask her this question: Do you intend to take your baby outside, and if so, will you only venture forth if the temperature outside is exactly the same as it is indoors? Common sense is all that is required!

Help in the home

If you are on your own or your husband cannot be at home with you, it is ideal if your mother can come and help, either right from the outset or to take over when/if your husband has to go back to work. It's helpful to remember that your mother looked after you when you were a baby and, although you might think that her views will be out of date, you may be surprised to find that a lot of her advice actually works! There is nothing like age and experience when it comes to dealing with babies.

You will almost certainly find your mother's presence very reassuring, and it will also be nice for you to have company during the day and to have someone to 'mother' and look after you by preparing meals and looking after your baby while you have an afternoon sleep.

I remember going to stay with my parents when my first baby was only a few weeks old. Even though I was a midwife, there were many occasions when my baby was crying and I didn't have a clue what to do! It was my mother who showed me how to settle my baby to sleep on my lap (when all other methods had failed), and she also taught me that sometimes it is in the best interests of a baby to be left to cry himself to sleep. Without my mother's help and advice in those early weeks, I think I would have been a nervous wreck and would have missed out on learning what I now consider to be fairly essential parenting skills. Granny sometimes knows best!

Maternity nurses

Most maternity nurses live in and are on duty 24 hours a day, six days a week. Many people assume that a maternity nurse is a trained nurse who has a specialist qualification in the care of newborns. This is rarely the case. Although some are qualified nurses, midwives or health visitors, most are simply experienced nannies who have chosen to work with new mothers. Before booking a maternity nurse you should:

- Interview her carefully to see whether her views on baby care reflect your own (e.g. is she pro- or anti-routine?)
- Ask about her qualifications and check her references.
- Agree in advance exactly what her duties will be. Most maternity nurses will only do things that directly involve the baby, but some are willing to do a bit more (e.g. help with the cooking and make cups of tea for your visitors).

- Find out how flexible she can be on her starting date. If in doubt, it's probably better to book her a week or two after your due date (as first babies are usually born later than expected), on the basis that you can probably survive initially with the help of your husband or mother.

A good and experienced maternity nurse should:

- Teach you how to do everything involved in the care of a newborn baby – changing nappies, bathing, swaddling etc.
- Help you to learn to differentiate between your baby's various cries, so you can tell whether your baby is crying because he is hungry, needs winding, is overtired etc.
- Show you how to sterilise bottles and make up feeds.
- Do the night feeds so you can catch up on your sleep.
- Help to guide (but not force) your baby into a good feeding and sleeping pattern.
- Boost your confidence so that you don't panic when she leaves!

Your maternity nurse should not:

- Force your baby into a strict and inflexible feeding routine. Although I am all in favour of aiming towards a good routine, it is not fair on the baby to be too strict in the early weeks.

- Be bossy and insist that everything be done her way or not at all! She can (and should) advise you, but ultimately, most, if not all, decisions concerning your baby should be made by you and your husband.
- Hog your baby and refuse to allow you and your husband to have any access to him in between feeds, on the basis that you will disrupt her routine with the baby. Unfortunately, some maternity nurses are inclined to do this.
- Undermine your confidence by continually disagreeing with you, the community midwife, health visitor etc.

Doulas

Doulas are proving to be an increasingly popular choice for mothers, possibly because they are cheaper and more flexible than maternity nurses. A doula is trained to provide emotional and practical support for new mothers and will usually have had the experience of bringing up her own children. She will normally do everything your own mother would do – help you feed, change nappies and bath the baby, as well as helping with household chores, shopping, cooking, and tending to your other children. She does not live in and you agree how often you want her to visit and for how long.

7 Settling into a Feeding Routine

Even when a baby is feeding and settling well, and is contented and gaining the right amount of weight, many mothers still worry whether they are doing everything right. Unfortunately, it is common for a mother to find that everyone tells her something different and, as a new mother may lack the confidence to trust her own judgement and instincts, it can be hard to know whose advice (if any!) to follow. This chapter covers all the questions that I have been asked over the years and, where appropriate, gives the different views that might be expressed.

Feeding on demand

Feeding on demand means being a bit flexible on feed times rather than insisting the baby conforms to a really strict routine. It does *not* mean you should feed your baby every time he cries, nor does it mean you should have no routine at all. Babies cry for all sorts of reasons and it is important to find out *why* he is crying, rather than automatically assuming that he is hungry and needs another feed. Babies are like toddlers – they thrive on regular meals and sleep times.

Most bottle-fed babies only need to feed once every three to four hours. If your baby needs to feed much more frequently than this, it is likely to be because:

- you are not offering him enough milk at each feed
- he has a medical problem such as reflux, that prevents him from being able to take enough milk at each feed
- he is suffering from excessive wind or colic, which keeps him awake (but does not mean he is hungry)

If you think it is better to feed totally on demand and not attempt to establish any routine at all, you should also be aware of the following:

- A baby will wake and cry for all sorts of reasons, of which hunger is only one. If you always assume that hunger is waking him you may end up feeding a baby who is crying with another problem (such as colic) which may be made worse if you feed him.
- A baby will suck on anything that you put in his mouth, so the fact that he drinks a bit of milk if you offer him the bottle does not necessarily mean that he was hungry.

- If you feed your baby every time he is a bit peckish rather than waiting until he is genuinely hungry, you will merely teach him to snack.

- It is hard for a mother to appreciate exactly what feeding on demand (using no guidelines) involves until she tries it. Only then will she realise that feeding two-hourly, for example, does not necessarily give her two hours free until the next feed. Feeds are timed from the point at which you start feeding, so, if a feeding session lasts an hour, she will only have a gap of one hour until the next feed. Feeding this often will make a mother as exhausted as her baby.

- A baby that is fed three- to four-hourly will usually start sleeping through the night sooner than a baby who is fed for weeks on end at totally random times, with his mother making no attempt to space out feeds.

These are some guidelines that may help:

1. Try not to feed within three hours of the previous feed

If your baby cries well before a feed is due, first see if you can settle him back to sleep by rocking his crib, gently patting his back and /or offering him a dummy. If this doesn't settle him, you could pick him up to see whether he needs winding or a nappy change and then try putting him down to sleep again. If you do manage to get him back to sleep you will have learnt the valuable lesson that a crying baby does not always need feeding. But if nothing settles him, you will have to feed him, but try to ensure it is a big feed rather than a little snack.

2. Try to feed your baby at least once every four hours during the day

During the first few weeks a baby needs at least six feeds during each 24-hour period – if a baby is not feeding three- to four-hourly during the day, he will need to feed more frequently at night to make up his milk intake. If you encourage him to feed more during the day (by waking him, if necessary) he is less likely to want to feed too often at night.

By following these two simple guidelines you should find that your baby will settle into a good feeding pattern and start sleeping through the night earlier than if he is left to his own devices.

Feeding on a strict four-hourly schedule (I do not recommend this)

In my experience mothers tend to fall into two main categories:

1. Those who are very relaxed and easy-going and who are perfectly prepared to feed their baby as and when he needs it,

without worrying too much when he feeds and when he sleeps – i.e. they are happy to take life as it comes.
2. Those who like routine and order in their lives, and want to get their babies onto a strict feeding routine right from the outset.

I think the middle road is best. Too lax an attitude to feeding and sleep times will often cause babies to become very unsettled and slow to sleep through the night; too strict a routine may not suit every baby and will create a lot of stress all round.

Weight gain
Monitoring your baby's weight is very important as this is the best indication as to whether he is getting enough food, and developing as he should.

- It is normal for a baby to lose up to 10 per cent of his birth weight in the first four days.
- If he loses much more than this you **must** give him more milk, either by offering him more at each feed or by feeding him more frequently.
- After day four, he should start gaining weight and be back to his birth weight by days 10–14.
- From then on his weight gain should roughly follow the centile chart in your Child Health Record booklet.

- Don't panic if your baby's weight gain is a bit uneven. Look at his general signs of contentment and overall weight gain.
- Although it is important that your baby gains weight fairly steadily, it will rarely do him any harm to go a week or two gaining slightly more or less weight than he should.
- An indication that your baby is underfed is if his stools change from mustard-yellow to green.
- If your baby's weight is falling *well* below the curve on his chart, you should consult a doctor.

When weighing your baby, you should take the following factors into account:

- His birth weight may have been inaccurately measured or recorded, and this will reflect on his subsequent weight measurements.
- A baby's weight at birth is usually affected by a combination of maternal diet and placental function, and does not necessarily reflect his eventual size. A baby born to small parents whose mother ate well during her pregnancy and had an efficient placenta could be quite large at first, but is then likely, at some stage, to slow his growth so that he will eventually end up a similar size to his parents. This will result in a slowing of weight gain at some point in his development and is both normal and expected.

- By the same token, a small baby born to large parents will almost certainly have a growth spurt at some point, resulting in his temporarily putting on more weight than the charts indicate he should.
- Scales are not always accurate, especially if different ones are used each time your baby is weighed. So don't panic if he doesn't appear to gain exactly the right amount of weight one week.
- It's best to weigh a normal baby (i.e. a full-term, healthy baby) no more frequently than once a week after day 10. This is because a baby's weight can fluctuate quite a bit each day depending on whether you weigh him before or after a feed, or before or after a wet nappy. For example, a baby who is weighed straight after a 90 ml (3 oz) feed will weigh 90 g (3 oz) more than if he had been weighed immediately before the feed.

You do not need to buy scales to weigh your baby. Your community midwife and health visitor will have all the necessary equipment.

Does my baby need extra water?
Neither a breast-fed nor a bottle-fed baby should need any extra water as milk provides all the fluid he requires. But you might occasionally want to offer some cool, boiled water if:

- the weather is particularly hot and your baby appears thirsty rather than hungry
- he is unsettled in between feeds
- he is constipated

Do be careful not to give so much water that your baby is then too full to take his milk feed. There are no calories in water, so you shouldn't give him water if he is hungry or if his weight gain is poor.

Should I wake my baby for a late-evening (10–11pm) feed?

From about six weeks onwards, many babies stop waking for the late-evening feed and gradually go longer until they need their next feed – this is the start of a baby being physically able to sleep through the night. At this point mothers face the dilemma: do they wake their baby for a 10pm feed in the hope that he will then sleep through until a civilised hour (6am, 7am or even 8am); or do they leave him to sleep and risk him waking shortly after they have gone to bed? Opinion on this is divided.

Theory one

You *should* continue to wake your baby for a late-evening feed to encourage him to start sleeping through the night from a young age. Babies who are not woken for this feed tend to be slower to sleep through the night and are also more likely to get into a habit of waking earlier in the morning, than babies who continue to be fed at 10pm for several months.

Theory two

You should *not* wake a baby for this feed as it is unfair to disrupt your baby's natural sleep pattern to suit your (rather than his) needs.

I don't think it matters either way and you should make a decision based on whatever works best for you and your baby. For example, some mothers are thrilled if their baby starts sleeping through the 10pm feed, while others would prefer to carry on doing the 10pm feed and have the longest sleep time taking place after this.

You can experiment to see what happens. If you wake your baby and he feeds well, settles back to sleep quickly and then sleeps longer as a result, it makes sense to continue waking him. But if your baby is hard to wake, feeds badly, takes ages to settle back to sleep, and then still wakes within a few hours it is better to leave him sleeping through the 10pm feed.

How to get your baby to sleep through the night

Many babies start going longer at night from about six weeks. Some do it earlier than this and others quite a lot later, but in general a baby will gradually reduce night feeds when he is physically ready to do so, providing he is getting plenty of milk during the day and has no problems (such as colic or reflux) that will disrupt his sleep. He is unlikely to drop an entire feed in one go, but instead will gradually last longer between feeds.

A baby who has established a good feeding pattern consisting of regular feeds and plenty of sleep between will usually sleep better at night than a baby who is being fed totally 'on demand' without any attempt being made to establish a routine. Thus, a baby who is feeding three- to four-hourly will generally sleep through the night sooner than a baby who is 'snacking' every hour or so and cat-napping throughout the day.

Remember this: a relaxed, well-fed baby will sleep longer and better than a tense, overtired baby.

To encourage night-time sleep

- Make sure that you are offering plenty of milk during the day.
- Try to space out feeds and organise your day so your baby is allowed to sleep in peace.
- Establish a routine whereby he is bathed, fed and settled quietly at a similar time each evening.
- Learn to recognise your baby's signals so you always put him down to sleep at exactly the right moment. If you put him down too early he won't be ready to drift off to sleep; if you leave it even a few minutes too late he will be overtired and will be equally unable to settle. This applies during the day as well as night.

- Put him in a quiet room to sleep in the evening.
- Distinguish between night and day by feeding your baby at night with the lights dimmed.
- Make sure that he is not getting cold at night – you may need to start using a sleeping bag during the winter months if he is coming out from under his blankets.
- Decide whether you want to wake him for a late-evening feed (see page 60) or let him sleep through.
- Offer him milk for the hungrier baby at the late-evening feed.
- Try diluting his middle-of-the-night feed by adding slightly less powder to encourage him to consume fewer calories at night and more during the day. *Never* add more powder than is recommended.

All of the above will work with most babies but be aware that:

- A very small or premature baby may need night feeds for a lot longer than a full-term baby.
- A baby suffering from reflux (or any other medical problem) will only sleep through when successful treatment makes him more comfortable and he can take larger feeds during the day.
- A small number of babies continue to wake at night for no obvious reason – you may just have to be patient.

I do not believe that you should try to force a baby to sleep through the night until he is six months old. After this almost all babies should be able to sleep through, so it is both reasonable and advisable to take firmer measures to achieve this if your baby is still waking – especially as it is easier to resolve bad sleeping habits in a young baby than a toddler. Tried and tested methods (such as 'controlled crying') are described in many other baby books – I do not plan to go into any more detail myself as this book is not intended to be a full child-care manual. (See 'Useful Resources', page 109, for recommended further reading.)

8 Bottle-feeding Problems

Most babies bottle-feed well but some don't. I see many babies who are feeding badly from the bottle and in most cases the mother had never thought to question the cause – she just assumed that her baby was naturally a very windy, messy or slow feeder. This section is aimed at these babies, and should help parents identify the cause and (hopefully!) find a solution.

Can't or won't suck efficiently
It is fairly common for a baby to be very slow and/or difficult to feed on the breast and this is one of many reasons why mothers give up breast-feeding. But some babies can also have problems with bottle-feeding and may:

- be very slow to feed, taking up to an hour to finish a bottle
- feed far too quickly, swallow too much air and/or posset large amounts of milk during and after feeds
- feed very noisily (see 'Laryngomalacia', page 106)

- be very 'messy', and spill a lot of milk out of the side of his mouth as he sucks
- refuse to take enough milk, and/or cry and fuss a lot during feeds

There are many reasons why a baby feeds badly from a bottle. Any of the following could be relevant:

- The bottle you are using doesn't suit him.
- He is very small or premature and needs time to develop a stronger sucking reflex.
- He has become dehydrated and has no energy to suck.
- He is jaundiced, which is temporarily making him too sleepy to feed well.
- He is naturally a very sleepy baby and/or a 'lazy' feeder.
- He has a minor defect in his mouth (e.g. tongue-tie or a high palate) which is preventing him from being able to suck efficiently – your GP or a paediatrician can check this for you.
- He is suffering from wind, colic or reflux, which is making him too uncomfortable to feed properly.
- He is suffering from milk allergy or intolerance.
- He suffered intracranial trauma at birth (minor damage to his head) which is affecting his sucking reflex – a cranial osteopath may be able to resolve this problem.

- He has an infection (e.g. of the urinary tract) that is making him too drowsy to feed properly – this needs diagnosing and treating.

By referring to the relevant sections in this book you should find that you can resolve most of the above issues. However, I do see many healthy full-term babies who are bad at feeding (breast or bottle) for no apparent reason – for these babies to feed better you will need to experiment with a number of bottles and teats before you discover which is best suited to their individual feeding difficulty.

Feeding too slowly
If your baby is feeding very slowly (i.e. taking far more than 20 minutes to finish his bottle), you need to use a faster flow teat. Do not assume that you are using the correct teat just because it is labelled as being suitable for the age of your baby – a week-old baby with a very weak suck needs a faster teat than a week-old baby with a very strong suck. Also, a baby with an exceptionally weak suck will usually feed better from a straight teat with a hole at the end, rather than from an orthodontic teat which has the hole at the top side of the teat. This is because a baby with a bad or weak sucking action will often clamp his mouth onto the teat instead of sucking on it – this seals the hole onto the roof of his mouth and prevents the milk from coming out. Always use as soft a teat as possible because the softer the teat, the less pressure the baby has to exert to get the milk.

Note: Cow & Gate make an excellent teat for premature babies (for hospital use only), which is made of soft latex with several large holes at the end to allow the milk to flow very quickly. This teat is not available in the shops, but your local hospital might be able to supply you with one or two if your baby clearly needs it. Alternatively, you could buy a latex teat and use a red-hot needle to enlarge the holes yourself.

Feeding too quickly

If your baby feeds far too quickly and/or is gulping and choking on the milk, you should change to a slower teat. You may need to experiment with different brands if you are already using the slowest teat available in the one you are using – this is because a slow flow in one brand can be twice as fast as the slowest flow in another brand. You could also try using a vari-flow teat (see 'Teats', page 4).

Messy feeders

Some babies are naturally messy feeders and will always need to be fed with bibs and muslins to hand! It is, however, worth experimenting with various bottles and teats to see whether your baby finds it easier to seal his mouth around a different design of teat. A baby who allows milk to dribble (or even squirt) out of the side of his mouth as he sucks on one teat, may feed without spilling even a drop of milk from another teat.

Note: I can't recommend any one bottle that will suit all babies, but I do find the Tommy Tippee bottle works well for most.

Possetting excessive amounts of milk
If your baby brings up large amounts of milk both during and after feeds it may be a sign of reflux, or he may simply be a messy feeder.

- Consult a doctor if he is showing other symptoms of reflux (see page 95).
- Try winding him more frequently.
- Experiment with different bottles and teats.
- If all else fails, ask your doctor whether he would recommend adding a thickening gel to his feeds. This is usually very effective but is really only for convenience rather than necessity – if your baby is happy and gaining weight, his excessive possetting is no cause for concern.

Note: I *did* use a thickening gel for my daughter, who brought up such vast amounts of milk that her clothing and bedding were permanently saturated in stale milk. Susan was not distressed when she vomited, but the gel made a huge difference to her comfort and my time spent washing all her clothing!

Refusing to take a bottle
This section is written for breast-feeding mothers who discover that they can't get their babies to drink anything out of a bottle. Babies who are bottle-fed from the outset will normally only become difficult to bottle-feed if they are unwell or develop a medical

problem such as reflux – and this is a totally different problem from that of a breast-fed baby who won't take a bottle at all.

It is very common for an exclusively breast-fed baby to refuse to take a bottle if he hasn't got used to taking one from a fairly early age, but unfortunately many mothers don't hear about this problem until it happens to them – by which time it's too late!

Most baby books gloss over the issue of bottle rejection, suggesting that it is a problem that can be solved simply by offering the baby a bottle on a regular basis and waiting for him to take to it in his own time. If only it were this simple! Unfortunately, the reality is that a large number of babies will become more (rather than less) resistant to the bottle as the weeks go by, and using this 'softly, softly' approach rarely works.

I am regularly consulted by mothers whose baby won't take a bottle, and most of them have very legitimate reasons (see below) for needing to introduce bottle-feeds. Because I see at first hand the trauma and distress that is created when a baby rejects the bottle, I regard this as a very important issue that needs addressing. I do not think it is cruel to teach a baby to feed from a bottle. Nor do I see any evidence that a baby suffers any lasting trauma when he is persuaded (against his will) to take a bottle, and the letters and phone calls I receive from the mothers confirm this.

Even if you intend to breast-feed until your baby is old enough to drink from a beaker, you should still tackle the issue of bottle rejection if at any point you discover that your baby won't drink from one. This is because there are many reasons why he might need to be given a bottle sooner than you planned and it will cause major problems if he is unwilling or unable to take one.

Any of the following problems could require your baby to be given a bottle:

- Your milk supply is low (and you have been unable to increase it), so your baby is permanently hungry and crying and waking a lot at night.
- Your baby's weight gain is poor and you are advised that you must give more milk. If you don't have enough breast milk (or your baby is not breast-feeding well) he will have to be given extra milk from a bottle.
- You are temporarily unable to breast-feed, perhaps because you are ill and/or have to go into hospital.
- You suffer a severe bout of mastitis, which temporarily or even permanently reduces your milk supply.
- You are due to return to work and you will not be able to breast-feed during your working hours.
- You have an important event to attend (e.g. a wedding) and would prefer to be able to leave your baby at home with a carer.

I don't know why some babies are so reluctant to feed from a bottle, but I can only assume that it's because they prefer the feel of their mother's breast and either don't want, or don't know how, to suck on a rubbery teat. I also get the impression that some babies are frightened of the bottle, either because the milk flows so differently and/or because they choked on one when it was first given and were immediately put off.

Regardless of the reason, bottle rejection is always very difficult to deal with and the older the baby becomes, the harder it is to resolve. It is much easier to persuade a baby under the age of three months to take a bottle than it is to persuade an older baby, and for this reason I do recommend that you tackle the problem head on as soon as it arises. In other words, if your baby first rejects the bottle when he is quite young, it is not a good idea to bury your head in the sand and hope the problem will go away. It won't! Instead, you should make a concerted effort there and then to get him to take a bottle and, if necessary, set aside a 24-hour period to do it.

There are no easy answers to this problem and what works with one baby will not necessarily work with another. However, the general principle involved is to get the baby to realise that there is something nice in the bottle! Hopefully you can achieve this by reading on.

There are two main types of bottle-rejecting babies:

- The ones who will happily sit for a good 10 minutes or so rolling the teat around under their tongue and from side to side in their mouth before deciding playtime is over and they want to be fed – at which point they start screaming.
- Those who go ballistic as soon as they see the bottle or as soon as the teat touches their lips. With these babies you will feel you have lost the battle before you even get past square one.

With both types of babies, the key to success is to try and get the baby to suck on the bottle by instinct (rather than desire), and then to make sure that he gets the milk quickly and easily and that he doesn't choke on it. To achieve this, you need to distract him so he doesn't notice you putting the bottle in his mouth, and then you hope that his automatic response is to start sucking.

This works with many babies, but others are not so easily duped and require a much firmer approach! You may need to spend at least an hour trying to get him to feed, he may cry a lot and you should also be prepared for it to take a full 24 hours before he accepts the bottle. I usually find I can get a baby to accept the bottle without too many tears, but even the ones who do cry are usually happily smiling at the end of the session – even if they are still refusing to feed and are still hungry. So, please don't worry if your baby resists and cries a lot, and be assured that he will come to no harm and will certainly harbour no grudge against you.

As some babies will hold out for the full 24 hours, you should only embark on the following robust approach if you are determined to see it through – if you give in within this time all your efforts will have been wasted and your baby will be even harder to convert to the bottle the next time you try.

- Set aside a 24-hour period during which time you will only offer your baby the bottle, i.e. no breast and no solid food.
- Try to choose a day when someone is around to help and support you, but you should be the one to feed your baby. Babies don't seem to react to the breast being so near (and yet so far!) and will usually feel more secure when handled by you.
- Don't give your baby anything at all to eat or drink for at least four hours before attempting to offer him a bottle. He must be hungry and want to feed.
- Have a variety of teats and bottles to hand, and experiment to see whether he appears to prefer one more than another. I have not found any one teat to be the miracle answer but with older babies (four months onwards) I have the most success using the Playtex orthodontic teat (because it is very short and hard, which makes it difficult for the baby to push out of his mouth); younger babies usually prefer a very soft teat (any make). I have never

managed (and therefore no longer try) to get a bottle-rejecting baby to use the Avent teats.

- Start by using a teat with a very fast flow so that milk pours into your baby's mouth without him needing to suck. I create my own fast-flow teat by using a hot needle to make the existing hole bigger – for this you need to use a latex teat. A fast-flow teat tends to work well with babies who scream as soon as the teat goes in their mouth, before they have even had a chance to realise that they are being given milk.

- It doesn't seem to matter what you put in the bottle (it's the bottle your baby is objecting to rather than its contents), but if you can use expressed breast milk at least you will know that your baby likes what you are offering him. If you can't manage to express enough milk (and/or get discouraged by the wastage if your baby won't drink it), formula milk is the next best thing to use. Babies tend to prefer formula milk to plain water, especially when they are hungry.

- Heat the milk so that it is as warm as possible, but not so warm that you risk burning your baby's mouth – breast-fed babies seem to like the milk to be very warm.

- Sit your baby bolt upright on your lap so that he won't choke and panic if the milk flow is too fast for him – you should not have him lying in your arms in the position you would adopt if you were breast-feeding him.

- Before putting the teat in your baby's mouth, try to attract his attention by waving rattles etc., then quickly put the teat in his mouth before he realises what you're doing. The theory behind this is that a baby will automatically suck on anything that goes in his mouth, provided he has not decided in advance that he doesn't want to. Ideally you would get someone else to wave the rattles, but if no one else is around you could try sitting with him in front of the television or anything else that will distract him.

- If your baby starts crying while you are trying to feed him, don't be put off – keep the teat in his mouth as this is the only way you will ever get him to suck on it. If you keep taking the teat out of his mouth, you will only upset him further and he will never learn that there is nice milk in the bottle.

- If he continues to cry, stand up and walk around with him while still keeping the teat in his mouth – many babies stop crying when you do this.

- If/when he starts sucking really strongly, you will probably need to change him on to a slightly slower teat to prevent him being overwhelmed by the milk flow.

- You may need to spend a minimum of one hour battling with your baby, but don't let his tears put you off. It is not cruel to do this to him and, if you have a deadline (i.e. you need to go back to work) he must learn to take his feeds from a bottle, however traumatic it seems at the time.

- If your baby falls into an exhausted sleep without having taken any milk, let him sleep and then start the whole process again when he wakes up. Keep on doing this until he realises that it is the bottle or nothing and decides he needs milk more than he needs your breast!

You can use the same bottle of milk for up to one-and-a-half hours, re-heating it as often as is necessary to keep it at an attractive temperature for him. Any milk that is left in the bottle after this time should be thrown away and a fresh bottle should be used for the next feeding attempt.

Most of the babies I see need only one session to get them happily on to the bottle and the majority of them continue to feed well from then on – it rarely happens that a baby feeds well with me and then refuses the next feed given by his mother at home. If, however, I fail to get a baby to take a *good* feed from the bottle, he will usually take a full feed at some point within the next 24 hours – so don't give up too soon.

For peace of mind, you might prefer to check with your GP before embarking on what could be a 24-hour marathon, but a normal healthy baby should come to no harm going without food for this long. After all, if you went under a bus tomorrow, your baby would not starve to death – he *would* take a bottle if that were his only option! I am aware that this sounds very harsh, but almost every week I see mothers for whom bottle rejection has become a real issue. Many of their babies are refusing to feed from a bottle even though they are clearly hungry and underweight, and in other cases the mother is becoming desperate because she is due to start back at work and feels she can't leave a baby who won't feed without her. I am convinced that the sooner this issue is resolved the better, and I also see how life is transformed for the whole family once the baby accepts the bottle. Everyone is happier.

Once your baby is happily taking a bottle, it is up to you to decide whether you can risk combining bottle-feeding and breast-feeding, or whether you feel that it's better to give up breast-feeding completely at this point. Most babies *are* perfectly happy to do a combination of the two, but I do occasionally come across some who revert to refusing a bottle as soon as they rediscover the breast. The choice (and risk) is yours!

This is a sample of just some of the letters that I have received, showing that most babies *are* happy taking a mixture of breast and bottle:

Dear Clare,

Thank you very much for your help in getting Mia to take a bottle. By the second feed at home she was sucking happily. It has taken a few days to get back into a routine but we are there now and she is even sleeping better at night … you have successfully transitioned us to the bottle, achieving in a few hours what I had failed to do over several weeks!

Thank you,
Kathy

Dear Clare,

I came to see you with my baby Charlie last month and you said you could not promise any miracles with a six-month-old bottle refuser. You *did* work a miracle: he starts nursery this week, a happy bottle-fed boy. I cannot thank you enough for taking the stress out of my imminent return to work.

Many thanks,
Imogen

Dear Clare,

Just a note to thank you *so* much for your invaluable and timely advice that you so willingly gave over the telephone on Thursday. After weeks of battling with little Rory with both the breast and bottle I was so grateful for such practical and hugely effective advice. I could not believe that I achieved in one feed what I had failed to do for weeks previously! Thank you again – what a relief!

Kind regards,
Diana

How to prevent bottle rejection (with your next baby!)
If you have been through the trauma of bottle rejection with one baby, you will want to make sure that it doesn't happen again. This is my advice:

- Do not listen to anyone who tells you that you must never give a breast-fed baby a bottle as this will cause 'nipple/teat confusion' and will ruin breast-feeding. There is little evidence to support this theory and I have never come across a baby who was happily and successfully breast-feeding, who then totally rejected the breast after being given a few bottles.
- Make sure that you introduce a bottle within the first three weeks or so of your baby's birth and then give the bottle as often as you think is necessary – probably about once every three to four days. At the first hint of your baby rejecting the bottle, you should use it at every feed until he is happily feeding from it again.
- To avoid a detrimental effect on breast-feeding, the bottles should contain expressed milk rather than formula. You can either express enough milk to give the entire feed via a bottle, or you can just express an ounce or two (30–60 ml), which you would give at the start of a feed, finishing with the breast.
- Although it might seem both time-consuming and annoying to give bottles when you're breast-feeding, I can assure you that

every minute you spend doing this will be time well spent if it avoids your baby rejecting the bottle at a later date.

- Don't assume that a baby who happily took a few bottles early on will still be willing to take a bottle if he then goes several weeks (or months) without having one.
- Be aware that it is very common for a baby to reject the bottle after a holiday without bottles (even if it was only a short one).

9 Common Medical and 'Baby' Problems

This chapter discusses the common medical problems that affect many babies. It also describes what I call 'baby' problems (such as poor weight gain), which don't necessarily have a medical cause but still need identifying and resolving.

Jaundice

It is very common and normal for a baby to become jaundiced within the first few days of birth, and in most cases this clears up of its own accord within two weeks without the need for any treatment. Jaundice occurs when there is more bilirubin in the blood than the liver can cope with, creating a build-up of bilirubin in the body, which turns the baby's skin and eyes yellow.

A baby is more likely to become severely jaundiced and need treatment if:

- he is very small or premature
- he suffered trauma and bruising during delivery (e.g. after a forceps or ventouse extraction)
- he becomes dehydrated because he is not feeding well

You do not need to worry if your baby is only mildly jaundiced and is feeding well, but you should contact your community midwife (or even take your baby back to hospital) if:

- the jaundice is increasing (i.e. your baby is becoming a darker yellow and it is spreading from his face and eyes down to the rest of his body)
- he is very sleepy, difficult to rouse and reluctant to feed
- he is showing signs of dehydration (see opposite)

Jaundice should always be taken seriously because very high levels of bilirubin can (very rarely) cause permanent brain damage.

If in doubt, you should take your baby to hospital for a blood test as this is the only completely accurate way of finding out whether his jaundice needs treating. If his bilirubin levels are too high, he will need to be admitted to hospital for a day or two for phototherapy.

If your baby is only mildly jaundiced, you should make sure that he is fed regularly (at least three- to four-hourly) until the jaundice fades.

Dehydration

A baby can quickly become dehydrated if he is not given enough milk, the formula feeds are too concentrated, or he suffers a prolonged bout of diarrhoea.

Signs of dehydration include:

- dry mouth and lips
- baby is drowsy and hard to wake
- he goes for more than six hours without passing urine
- his urine is dark and has a strong smell
- tiny orange or pink crystals (urates) appear in his nappy
- he has a sunken fontanelle (the soft bit on the top of his skull where the bones have not yet fused)

If your baby is showing signs of dehydration you should try to give him more milk, making sure you are mixing the feed with the correct ratio of powder and water. If your baby doesn't quickly improve (by passing more urine and becoming more alert) you should ring your doctor or even take him straight to hospital. Mild (and temporary) dehydration is not a worry but severe dehydration can be harmful to your baby and needs immediate attention.

The sleepy baby
Some babies are naturally calm and sleepy and often have to be woken for feeds – this is normally a bonus rather than a cause for concern! But you should consult a doctor if:

- your baby is very jaundiced
- he is not passing urine regularly and/or his urine is dark and smelly
- he is so sleepy that he won't feed properly
- he remains abnormally sleepy and is not gaining the right amount of weight (this baby may have an infection – e.g. of the urinary tract – that requires treatment)

The unsettled baby
Just as some babies are naturally sleepy and relaxed, others are naturally tense and unsettled and need skilled parenting to help them go to sleep. Hunger is the main reason why a breast-fed baby is hard to settle, but physical problems are the more likely cause of a bottle-fed baby being unsettled.

If your baby is only unhappy for a small part of the occasional day, you may simply have a baby who requires a bit more attention at these times. But if he regularly cries every time you put him down, you should try to discover the cause of his distress, rather than just assuming that he is a 'difficult' baby.

- Check that you are giving him enough milk. (You may need to use a faster-flow teat if he is a slow feeder and falling asleep too soon.)
- Are you are using the right bottle for him? You may need to experiment with different bottles and teats to see which suits him best.
- Try a different brand of formula.
- Make sure you are winding him properly.
- Swaddle him, offer him a dummy and rock him to sleep, rather than simply putting him down and leaving him to settle on his own.
- Try Infacol, gripe water or Colief if you think he is suffering from wind or colic.
- Consult a doctor if you suspect milk allergy or reflux.
- Consider homeopathy or cranial osteopathy (see page 107).

Despite all the above tips, I am well aware that some babies will always be hard to settle and no amount of expertise will immediately transform them into an 'easy' baby. I regularly visit mothers who have a tense baby and I always wish I could wave a magic wand and perform miracles – but I can't! Instead, I offer tried and tested strategies and reassure them that their baby will eventually become easier, even if there is no instant solution.

How to settle your baby on your lap
If your baby has become really fraught and overtired, settling him to sleep on your lap is a good solution. This method works far better than endlessly pacing the room, swapping your baby from shoulder to shoulder and continually putting him down as soon as he dozes off, only to find he is awake again within minutes. The real key to the success of the 'lap' method is that it tends to send your baby into a deeper and more permanent sleep than other methods and it can be done whenever you can't, or don't want to, go out with the pram. It works extremely well with babies up to the age of about three months, but babies older than this will usually settle best when taken for a long walk in a pram.

Step one
Sit comfortably with someone or something (e.g. the television!) to keep you company so that you don't try to rush things. Place a pillow on your lap and your baby on his tummy on the pillow, turning his head gently to one side so that you can, if necessary, put a dummy in his mouth (see page 34). You should then start patting your baby on his back just above the nappy level, firmly and rhythmically, at a rate of approximately one pat per second. Most babies find this very soothing and comforting and will usually fall asleep quite quickly. Don't be discouraged if he cries a lot for the first few minutes because, if you persist with the rhythmic

patting, you should find that his crying will diminish and he'll start to fall asleep.

Once your baby is asleep, you can stop patting him but you should leave him lying on your lap for a few minutes longer to check that he is sound asleep and has not just dozed off. If he starts stirring and waking, pat him again (but do not pick him up) until he goes back to sleep. If he stays asleep for approximately five minutes after you have stopped patting him, you can pick him up gently and put him into his crib.

Hopefully he will remain asleep, but if he does wake up, you will need to put him back on your lap and start the process all over again.

Step two

If your baby wakes every time you move him to his crib, you may need to leave him sleeping on the pillow until his next feed is due. Gently lift the pillow from your lap and put it (and your baby) on a surface where he will be safe (e.g. on a sofa, surrounded by cushions) and where he will not be at risk of rolling off.

Step three

If your baby is so tense and overtired that he wakes every time you move the pillow, you will have to spend an hour or more sitting with him asleep on your lap. Although this is very restricting for you, it is a great deal more relaxing than the alternative of pacing around with your baby over your shoulder. You may also find that you only need to do this after one or two feeds to break the cycle of 'overtiredness' and from then on your baby will be able to settle himself.

It is safe to leave your baby to sleep on his tummy during the day, provided you are around to keep an eye on him. Do not leave him unattended.

Colic

Colic is the term used to describe the pain a baby suffers when he gets griping spasms in his small intestine, which can happen before, during and after feeds. Colic affects both breast- and formula-fed babies and there is no known cause or treatment. It usually starts round about the third week and lasts for three to four months before clearing up of its own accord. Coping with a colicky baby is extremely stressful for the whole family (as well as your baby), and it is therefore essential to get a proper diagnosis to be sure that colic really is the cause of your baby's distress.

Although colic affects a lot of babies, it is often misdiagnosed, usually by family or friends, but also by health visitors, GPs, etc., many of whom assume that all crying babies have colic! Many of the babies I see are in fact suffering from hunger (particularly when breast-fed), reflux or milk allergy. **Please exclude these problems before assuming your baby has colic.** (See pages 95 and 104.)

Signs and symptoms

- The baby usually feeds well from the bottle (often falling asleep at the end of the feed) but wakes shortly after you put him down.
- He appears to have been woken by a sudden griping pain.
- As he cries, he may either draw his legs up to his stomach or hold them out so his whole body goes rigid.
- His abdomen may feel tense and swollen.
- Winding may help a bit but does not solve the problem (because the pain of colic is caused by a combination of wind and bowel spasms).
- He will stop crying if you cuddle him, rock him in a cradle or bouncing chair, or take him for a walk in the pram.
- He wakes and starts crying again almost as soon as you put him down or stop walking him in the pram.

Although you cannot cure colic, there are ways of making it more bearable for both you and your baby:

- Experiment with different bottles and teats. The Doctor Brown bottle may help.
- Slow down! Take time to wind and cuddle your baby, then swaddle him, offer a dummy and rock him to sleep.
- Try using the various over-the-counter remedies that are available from the chemist (e.g. gripe water, Infacol or Colief).

Although some of these can be quite effective, don't be discouraged if you find that what seems to work at some feeds doesn't work at others.

- Ask your doctor if he can prescribe an anti-spasmodic medicine.
- Try not to feed your baby within three hours of the start of the previous feed. If you keep putting milk into his tummy, his colic is likely to become worse.
- Carry him around in a sling or take him for long walks in his pram.
- Check that his clothing is not too tight – trousers with an elastic waistband will be more uncomfortable than a babygro, dungarees etc.
- Accept offers of help from friends and family.
- Try homeopathy or cranial osteopathy.
- Settle him using my 'lap' method. (See page 88.)

Remember: if all else fails, your baby will eventually grow out of colic – usually at around three to four months.

Evening colic / evening fretting
It is very common for babies to be unsettled in the evening, usually from about 6pm to 11pm or midnight, and this is often caused by colic which, for some reason, only occurs during this part of the day. Although it is very wearing to have a baby that needs a lot of attention every evening, you should try to think positively and

consider yourself lucky if this is the only time of day that he suffers from colic.

Although the methods described above may help, there's not much you can do to cure a baby who is genuinely suffering from evening colic. Try not to get too stressed, accept any offers of help from your husband, and remember that your baby will grow out of it eventually.

Constipation

Although constipation is more common amongst bottle-fed babies than breast-fed babies, it normally only affects a small percentage of babies. A baby is only considered to be constipated if he goes several days without opening his bowels, is suffering colicky pains, visibly strains to pass the motion and then produces hard, pellet-shaped stools.

You can:

- try him on a different brand of formula, but if this doesn't help, don't keep changing brands without first consulting your health visitor or doctor
- offer him cool, boiled water between feeds
- add a teaspoon of brown sugar to the water
- give him an ounce or two of diluted prune juice or freshly squeezed orange juice

If his constipation is only temporary and easily resolved with these home remedies, there is nothing further that needs to be done, but if it persists you should consult a doctor.

Anal stenosis

A very small number of babies have a tight anal sphincter muscle (anal stenosis) which makes it harder for them to pass motions, even though the stools are soft. Your baby may have anal stenosis if he is uncomfortable and colicky and keeps visibly straining to do a dirty nappy, but then produces soft stools. Treatment is very simple and involves gently dilating the sphincter muscle – this can be done by your GP or paediatrician.

Thrush

Thrush is a fungal infection caused by the yeast organism *Candida albicans*, which normally lives harmlessly on the skin or in various parts of the body such as the vagina, mouth or bowel. This yeast is usually kept at bay by 'harmless' bacteria and a healthy immune system, but if a baby has a weak immune system or is prescribed a course of antibiotics (which will destroy these bacteria) the fungus will flourish and give rise to thrush.

It is fairly common for a mother and/or her baby to get thrush, and it is easily transmitted between mother and baby and everyone else in the household. (If you have thrush on your nipples and are giving some breast-feeds, you will both need to be treated, even if only one of you has symptoms.) You should be meticulous with hygiene and pay particular attention to sterilising dummies and teats etc.

Signs of thrush in the baby:

- white spots in his mouth
- a creamy white coating on his tongue, usually on the back half, which does not rub off (milk will rub off)
- he keeps pulling off the bottle because his mouth is sore
- he is fretful and difficult to settle
- nappy rash that does not heal

If you think your baby has thrush you should see your GP, who will be able to make a diagnosis and prescribe a suitable treatment – usually Daktarin oral gel or Nystatin drops, which you apply to your baby's mouth after feeds.

Gastro-oesophageal reflux

This is a fairly common condition that affects many babies but frequently goes undiagnosed. Reflux happens when a baby has a weak sphincter muscle at the top of his stomach, which can then allow milk and acidic gastric juices to go back up into his oesophagus rather than staying in his stomach. This gives the baby the equivalent of acid heartburn every time he feeds – and the bigger the feed, the more pain he will suffer.

Many people (including doctors) will only consider reflux as a possibility if the baby is bringing up some or most of his feeds, but in reality, many babies can have severe reflux without ever being seen to vomit up milk. Instead, the milk just goes up and down in the oesophagus, with the stomach acid 'burning' and damaging the delicate tissue that lines the oesophagus – this 'silent' reflux is usually far more painful than visible reflux.

You should consider reflux if your baby is showing any of the following signs:

- He starts each feed sucking eagerly and well, but then suddenly starts crying and pulling away from the bottle.
- He may throw his head back and arch his back. His whole body may become rigid and it often takes several minutes to calm him down.
- Once calm, he may attempt a few more sucks but will quickly start crying again and refuse to continue feeding, even though he has only taken a small amount of milk.
- He cries after the feed if you try to lie him down and he will only stop crying when you hold or sit him upright.
- He brings up more milk after each feed than you would expect with a normal posset.

- He consistently takes small feeds, which last him less than three hours.
- His weight gain is poor but he won't drink more milk.

Although some babies suffer from reflux at birth (and are therefore difficult to feed from the outset), the majority of babies gradually become worse at feeding, with the symptoms becoming more obvious from about six weeks onwards. At this point, diagnosis becomes easier.

- The most obvious effect of reflux is that a baby will regularly (but not always) refuse to drink as much milk as he should be taking for his age and size.
- A reflux baby will usually happily drink 60–90 ml (2–3 oz) and then start crying, arching his back and refusing to finish the bottle.
- By six weeks, the average baby needs much more than this – a minimum of 120 ml (4 oz) per feed but more likely 150–180 ml (5–6 oz) depending on his weight.
- As a baby gets older and needs larger amounts of milk, the discrepancy between what your baby will take and what he should be taking becomes much more obvious.

If you think your baby has reflux, you should consult your GP to have the diagnosis confirmed. In obvious cases of reflux, your GP will usually prescribe Infant Gaviscon and he may also recommend you change to a special anti-reflux formula milk. If your baby improves dramatically on Gaviscon, no further treatment or tests should be necessary and he can remain on it until such time as your GP considers that it is no longer needed.

If your baby does not respond to Gaviscon or there is doubt about the diagnosis, your GP may arrange for him to go into hospital for tests, which are fairly simple and should not be too distressing for you or your baby. Depending on the results, your baby may then be prescribed an antacid such as Ranitidine or an inhibitor such as Losec, which can stop acid production altogether. Unfortunately, reflux is not always cured overnight and I'm afraid that it occasionally involves many weeks of misery (for both of you) before the right mix of drugs is found and the symptoms of reflux abate. If this does happen, try to comfort yourself with the knowledge that every baby will eventually grow out of reflux, with or without treatment.

Because babies with reflux need to be kept upright as much as possible (to help keep the milk down in the stomach), your baby will feel a bit more comfortable if you:

- feed him in an upright position
- keep him sitting upright for at least half an hour after feeds
- tilt his cot by propping it up at the head end

Note: If your baby does not respond well to treatment for reflux and continues to be unable to take in enough milk for his needs, it might be a good idea to start him on solids earlier than usual (i.e. well before six months). You could discuss this with your GP or paediatrician.

The following letter illustrates perfectly what happens when reflux goes undiagnosed:

Dear Clare,

Thank you for your advice about my baby Jack, who I was having problems feeding. When I told you that during a 24-hour period of feeding him with a bottle he always seemed to have some difficulty at 3 oz, you said you were sure that he was suffering from reflux.

I was, however, persuaded by my two GPs, my mother, my mother-in-law, three health visitors and a paediatrician that he was actually suffering from wind/colic and that 3 oz was simply his stomach capacity at 4–6 weeks.

Nightmarishly, as he got older his problems, rather than abating, got worse and worse. As you warned correctly, without treatment reflux can become a serious problem. I am now in the terrible predicament of practically not being able to feed him at all – I had to take him to hospital two days ago, and I am now pleased when he takes even half an ounce.

I feel so idiotic for not following your advice, because if I had I may not be in the position I am in now. Surrounded by conflicting advice I simply didn't know what to do. I did actually try Gaviscon but I was told to give it to him at the end of a feed and therefore thought it was pointless because a) he wouldn't take it because he was full and b) it made no difference because all the problems happened during the feed.

I have been given Ranitidine and Domperidone and have been giving him Gaviscon before the feeds. So far there is no improvement and I am obviously desperate. I have an appointment with a paediatrician next week, but I am continuously on the verge of going back to A&E as I am terrified he is dehydrated.

I would like to stress for any new, inexperienced mother that when doctors tell you that 'reflux is the flavour of the month at the moment', you must insist on a second opinion or somehow persuade them that this is really a problem. One doctor even carried out a post-natal depression questionnaire on me when I went back to her for the third time trying to convince her my baby had reflux. In all honesty I actually don't know what I could have done otherwise, except refuse to be fobbed off as I was.

I'd also like to add that apart from his feeding problems Jack has become an adorable baby, mostly calm and smiley between feeds, with no weight gain problems except for over the last three weeks (probably because our feeds went on for hours as I kept putting him back on the breast again and again, desperate to keep him latched on for a few minutes – another thing doctors insisted was my fault).

Thank you, Clare, for your help; if only the other health professionals had been as knowledgeable as you I may not be in this horrendous situation today.

Best regards, Hattie

Poor weight gain

Some babies fail to put on enough weight but are happy and contented, while others are under-weight and are clearly both unhappy and hungry. If your baby is happy and contented, his failure to put on weight may be due to his individual make-up and be nothing to worry about. A baby like this will often have a growth spurt and suddenly put on a lot of weight in a short space of time. But if your baby is not happy and settled and appears to be hungry, you need to discover the cause and do something about it.

Check that you are offering your baby enough milk

I know this appears obvious, but I have seen many a mother who is consistently giving too little milk to her baby and is then absolutely amazed when I point out that her baby is hungry! I find that this most often happens when a baby is born prematurely and the mother is initially given strict guidelines on how much milk her baby should have at each feed, but isn't then told that she should increase the amount as he gets older. Start by offering your baby extra milk at each feed, but if he doesn't want, or can't manage, larger feeds, try introducing an extra feed during the day to see whether this suits him better. If he takes more milk and his weight gain improves, your problem is solved.

Exclude medical problems

If you are offering your baby plenty of milk but he won't drink it, you should consult your GP. The most common reason why a baby won't drink enough milk for his needs is physical discomfort caused by conditions such as colic, milk intolerance or allergy, reflux or (very rarely) a tight anal sphincter muscle. If your baby is suffering from any of these conditions, early diagnosis and treatment will enable him to drink more milk and gain weight, thus making life infinitely better for both you and your baby.

Excessive weight gain

A lot of mothers think that it's impossible to over-feed a baby because he will always stop feeding when he's had enough. Unfortunately, this is not true. It is in fact easy to over-feed a bottle-fed baby because you can see how much he is drinking and it is therefore very tempting to try to persuade him to finish all his bottles (especially if it's the last feed of the day) in the mistaken belief that he will sleep longer. If you regularly give your baby more milk than he actually needs, he will almost certainly put on too much weight.

If your baby is gaining too much weight:

- Do not expect him to drink an identical amount of milk at every feed and don't persuade him to finish all his bottles.
- Use a slower teat if your baby feeds too quickly and is possibly demanding more milk for the comfort of sucking rather than hunger.
- Try distracting him when he finishes a bottle by walking around with him for a bit – this will allow time for the message to get through from his stomach to his brain to say he's full!
- Change him to formula milk for the hungrier baby. (See page 11.)
- Try mixing his milk with one less scoop of powder (this will still make him feel full, but he will be getting fewer calories). Never make the feed more concentrated by adding extra powder.
- Don't assume that your baby is hungry every time he cries – he may simply be tired or in need of entertaining. After about six weeks, babies spend more time awake and require more stimulation.

If your baby continues to pile on the weight despite your efforts to reduce his milk intake, you should probably just relax and accept that you have a very hungry baby, who is temporarily going through a growth spurt or is growing to match his parents (see 'Weight gain', page 57). Allow him to have as much milk as it takes to keep him happy and contented, and be aware that you may need to start him on solids before six months – because solid food will satisfy him more than milk, while providing fewer calories. Ask your GP's advice on this.

Milk allergy / milk intolerance

There is no known cause of milk allergy but it often runs in families. When a baby is allergic to milk, his immune system over-reacts by producing antibodies, which cause a variety of symptoms (see below). The immune system then gives a rapid antibody response every time the baby is fed milk, causing the symptoms to become more immediate and more severe the longer he is exposed to it.

Milk intolerance occurs when the baby finds it hard to digest milk – it does not involve the immune system, so the symptoms are less severe.

Signs and symptoms

- Your baby is colicky, crying and unsettled.
- He has abdominal pain and bloating.
- He suffers diarrhoea or constipation.
- He develops skin rashes or eczema.
- He has swelling around the lips or a runny nose.
- He is difficult to feed and settle and may vomit up his feeds.

If your baby is showing any of these signs and symptoms, you should consult a doctor to get a proper medical diagnosis. If your baby does have a milk allergy or intolerance, his symptoms will usually subside quickly once he is prescribed a hypo-allergenic formula milk. Most babies will eventually grow out of a milk allergy.

Lactose intolerance

Lactose is a sugar present in both breast and formula milk. It needs to be broken down by an enzyme in the bowel called lactase to allow the milk to be absorbed easily. But if a baby has little or no lactase (this can often result from a bout of gastro-enteritis) the milk is hard to digest and he may suffer from excessive wind, abdominal distension and pain, diarrhoea, frothy stools and vomiting.

If your baby is diagnosed with lactose intolerance he will need to switch to a specialist formula milk, which you may be able to get on prescription from your doctor.

Tongue-tie

A baby is described as being 'tongue-tied' when the membrane that attaches the tongue to the floor of the mouth is too short and tight, and extends too far towards the tip of the tongue. This prevents the tongue from moving freely, which can make it difficult for a baby to feed easily from the breast and sometimes from the bottle too. If your baby is clearly affected by tongue-tie, you should discuss it with your doctor, who may suggest that you get the tongue-tie clipped. This is painless and simple to do.

Laryngomalacia

If your baby has abnormally noisy breathing, especially when feeding, he may be suffering from laryngomalacia. This is a condition where the larynx and/or the surrounding areas are under-developed and floppy.

Signs and symptoms

- The baby makes a high-pitched crowing or rattling sound on inspiration, which is usually more noticeable when he is crying, feeding or lying on his back.
- He may have difficulty in feeding and/or breathing.

Most babies grow out of this condition without needing any treatment, but you should consult a doctor if your baby is struggling to feed and is not gaining weight.

Note: Many babies with laryngomalacia also suffer from reflux.

Baby bottle tooth decay

Baby bottle tooth decay is a serious condition that can destroy your child's primary teeth when they start coming through at about six months. It occurs when teeth are frequently exposed to liquids containing sugar, such as formula milk, breast milk, cows' milk and fruit juice. When bottle-feeding, the milk pools around your baby's teeth, providing food for decay-producing bacteria, which then form acids that damage the tooth enamel. To stop this happening, it is important to start teaching your baby to take some of his feeds from a special cup at about six months and to stop bottle-feeding completely by the age of a year.

Cranial osteopathy
Osteopathy can be very successful in treating tense, irritable and unsettled babies, colic, feeding difficulties (on breast or bottle), and sleeping problems. Although cranial osteopathy is very gentle and non-invasive, it is best to consult your GP before seeing an osteopath to rule out normal reasons for your baby's symptoms. Many babies will improve simply by changing the way you feed or handle them. It is also important to exclude medical conditions (such as reflux) before going down the road of alternative treatments for your baby.

Osteopathy can be very effective for:

- A crying, irritable baby who rarely settles well in between feeds, even though all his needs appear to have been met. He may be jumpy and react badly to loud noises. He may need to be held and cuddled a lot as he is unable to relax and go to sleep on his own.

- A baby who feeds badly from the bottle, maybe taking up to an hour to feed, even when using a teat with a fast flow. He may also feed noisily and messily and swallow a lot of air, causing him to suffer from excessive wind.
- A baby suffering from colic.
- A 'sicky' baby who regularly possets more than is usual.
- A baby with marked asymmetry of the head that persists long after the birth.

Useful Resources

Books
New Toddler Taming by Dr Christopher Green
This is a brilliant book. It is easy to read and contains fantastic advice on all aspects of baby- and childcare. It also has an excellent section on sleep problems.

The New Contented Little Baby Book by Gina Ford
For those who would like to follow a more routine-based, step-by-step guide to caring for their baby, Gina Ford has proved invaluable to many mothers.

A Perfect Start by Christine and Peter Hill
This book (written by my colleagues) provides sound practical advice that is ideal for anxious new parents.

Other Information
Babylist
50 Sulivan Road
London SW6 3DX
Tel: 020 7371 5145
Gives independent, unbiased advice to help you choose baby
equipment and nursery items.

www.britishdoulas.co.uk
Tel: 020 7244 6053
Provides information about hiring a doula.

About the Author

Clare Byam-Cook trained as a nurse at Westminster Hospital and qualified in 1976. After going on to do a midwifery course at Pembury Hospital in Kent and qualifying as a midwife in 1979, she then worked for four years at Queen Charlotte's Hospital in London until the birth of her first baby. In 1989 Clare was approached by ante-natal teacher Christine Hill to join Hill's Chiswick practice as her breast-feeding specialist and she has been there ever since.

During her years working with Christine Hill, Clare has gained invaluable experience in everything to do with breast-feeding, bottle-feeding, crying babies (and crying mothers!), and everything else associated with the day-to-day care of newborn babies. In addition to teaching at the ante-natal classes, she makes home visits to any mother who asks for her help, and says she has learnt more about babies and feeding problems from doing these home visits than in all her years spent working as a hospital midwife.

Clare has gained a reputation for being able to solve almost any breast-feeding problem and all her clients come to her by word-of-mouth referral from their friends, GPs, obstetricians, paediatricians, midwives and health visitors. Clare has never advertised her services and says that when the referrals dry up she knows it will be time for her to retire!

Clare feels that there is no better experience to be acquired than by being in a position to see the same problems time and time again. As a result, most of the advice she gives in this book is based on the knowledge she has gained during the many years she has been doing these home visits. It is not based solely on textbook theories.

Index